Peter Eckart

SIMPLICITY FOR SUCCESS IN BUSINESS

To the Rinconada Team —
this was written here to
a large extent. —
Thanks so much for the
great times —.

All the best,

PALO ALTO, CA
JULY 2020

SIMPLICITY
FOR SUCCESS
IN BUSINESS

ESSENTIALS
The Best of Silicon Valley & McKinsey

PETER ECKART

Simplifier Inc.

To my Daniel

*This book is for you from your dad
to show you how you can use
Simplicity for your success
and, most importantly,
happiness in your life!*

First published in the United States by Simplifier Inc., 2020

Library of Congress Control Number: 2020906581

ISBN 978-1-7348649-7-7 (paperback)
ISBN 978-1-7348649-0-8 (pdf)
ISBN 978-1-7348649-1-5 (kindle)

Printed in the United States of America

Set in Lora and Catamaran
Quotes by Ken Segall with kind permission
Design by Daniela Chervenkova and Andrey Chervenkov

TABLE OF CONTENTS

INTRODUCTION
"IT'S NOT ROCKET SCIENCE"

"It's *not rocket science* ..." You've undoubtedly heard this expression often and in many different contexts. It's another way of saying, "It's *not complicated; it's much simpler than you may think!*" Being a rocket scientist-turned-management-consultant, I have used this expression many times. Typically, I follow up with, "*Trust me, I know — I am a rocket scientist!*" Which usually gets a laugh.

But in many instances, even though my clients are laughing, I get the impression that they don't quite believe me. I am trying to assure them not to worry and that tackling the challenge at hand is quite straightforward. Still, I sense that what they are really thinking is more along the lines of, "*This is obviously a complex problem, so finding a solution will be difficult,*" or "*Our challenge is absolutely unique, so it requires a unique solution.*" So — am I just being cheeky, or am I serious about the not-being-rocket-science bit?

Holding this book in your hands, you can already tell that I'm very serious. What prompted me to write it was the realization that you can leverage the power of *Simplicity* across many professions and industries. *Simplicity* in teaching, problem-solving, or communications can move mountains. I've experienced this throughout my professional life: as a space engineering professor, a management consultant (working for clients both at McKinsey & Co. and my own firm), and in various executive and advisory roles. By sharing my experiences in this book (and future volumes of the *Simplicity for Success* series), my key objective is to help you understand the power of *Simplicity* and learn how to apply it for your success.

Peter Eckart
Palo Alto, CA
March 2020

UNDERSTANDING
THE POWER OF SIMPLICITY

CHAPTER 1

MY PERSONAL SIMPLICITY JOURNEY

"TRUTH IS EVER TO BE FOUND IN SIMPLICITY,
AND NOT IN THE MULTIPLICITY
AND CONFUSION OF THINGS."

—ISAAC NEWTON

My first encounter with the power of Simplicity came when I met my future Ph.D. advisor while still in high school. Through a series of coincidences (destiny calling!), I found myself listening to a presentation by space engineering professor Harry O. Ruppe. He had conducted NASA's first human Mars mission studies at the Marshall Space Flight Center in Huntsville, Alabama, in the early 1960s. Amazingly, I understood pretty much everything he was talking about during his presentation. What I found astounding that day, was that a university professor was explaining rocket science in simple enough terms for a high school student to understand.

Not too long after that, I had the great fortune to

be a relatively frequent guest at the home of Hermann Oberth, then in his early nineties. Oberth, a German, was one of the three founding fathers of modern rocketry and astronautics, along with a Russian, Konstantin Tsiolkovsky, and an American, Robert Goddard.

In 1922, Oberth finished his doctoral dissertation in which he describes how to design a space launch system. The core of his work is the rocket equation, a simple formula that explains how to accelerate a rocket such that it can reach Earth orbit. Oberth also postulated that it should be possible for humans to travel into space and create commercial businesses related to space flight. His work was inspired by his reading of Jules Verne's book *From the Earth to the Moon* when he was a teenager.

The University of Heidelberg in Germany rejected his dissertation as 'utopian.' Fortunately, Oberth was pushed by his wife who used some of the family's savings to privately publish his work in 1923. The *Rocket into Planetary Space* was given as a birthday present to a teenage boy named Wernher von Braun. He later built the Saturn V rocket that carried Neil Armstrong and Buzz Aldrin to the surface of the Moon on July 20, 1969. Oberth was present at the launch of the Apollo 11 mission.

When I was having lunch with Oberth sometime in the mid-1980s, I asked him how he came up with his key concepts and how he felt about the initial rejection of his work. Oberth shrugged and said, "Well, you know, all I ever did was to simply write down what I knew is right." This simple sentence became one of the guiding stars of my life — I also wanted to 'simply write down what I know is right.'

Years later, my other Ph.D. advisor, space engineering professor H. Hermann Koelle, who had developed the concept for the Saturn launcher family, gave me some great advice when I started writing my own doctoral dissertation. He said, "*Write the conclusions first.*" This simple, counter-intuitive suggestion turned out to be as powerful as it was hard to implement. As I would later understand, he introduced me to what top-management consultancy, McKinsey & Co., calls the *hypothesis-driven approach* in a business context. (More on this later ...)

After spending the initial years of my professional life as a space engineering professor, I was seeking a new challenge. I decided to leave academia to enter the world of management consulting. However, I had absolutely no idea whether I would be up to the challenge, especially given that I did not have an MBA.

I called an old friend who had studied aerospace engineering with me and who had recently been promoted to Partner at McKinsey & Co. My simple question to him was, "*You know me well, so do you think that I would be up to the challenge of becoming a management consultant?*" After an hour-long conversation, he gave me some succinct advice: "*As long as you keep in mind that Profit equals Revenue minus Cost, you are in good shape.*" That simple? Excellent — I was up for the challenge! I applied and indeed landed a job with McKinsey & Co.

Over the years, I have been blessed with many outstanding teachers, mentors, and colleagues. The common denominator between all of them was that they all truly understood the fundamentals of their respective subject matter — be it in space engineering, business, or elsewhere.

This understanding enabled them to explain both the fundamentals and specific aspects of their subject areas to others in simple terms. It also helped them to prioritize and focus on critical issues rather than wasting their time (and that of others) with 'side topics.' Which, in turn, enabled others, like me, to understand what's important and focus on that.

Over the past two decades, I worked not only for McKinsey & Co., but also in different senior roles in 'line jobs' before deciding to set up my own management consultancy. I worked across numerous industries, on three continents, for some of the largest corporations in the world, a major family business, mid-size companies, governments, and even a unicorn start-up.

Quite frequently, I came across the notion that people in a specific industry or business saw their challenges as unique or industry-specific. By and large, I found that this is not the case. While, of course, different industries and different companies face particular situations, most challenges or processes are very similar across all businesses, large or small. Hence, I am convinced that the power of *Simplicity* can be applied to any business.

As I developed the idea of writing this book, I decided to conduct some comprehensive research on *Simplicity* and fundamental business concepts and tools.

In a first step, I explored what others had to say about the concepts, tools, and value of *Simplicity*. I found very few fellow believers in and promoters of *Simplicity*. Only about a dozen books are available that focus on this topic (you can find the titles in the *References* section at the end of this book — if you know others, please let me know). Most of these volumes look at a particular angle of *Simplicity*:

- Some focus on case examples and why simplicity is so powerful
- Some focus on specific areas, such as design or decision making
- Some provide mostly tactical tools, for example, for communications and process design

Yet, no one has taken a holistic look at *Simplicity* from the perspective of a business leader. Hence, I decided to write a book based on a framework that looks at all relevant business functions and needs across three buckets:

- Planning
- Products & Services
- People

Besides, I identified two complementary areas that we will discuss. Both are crucial success factors in today's business world:

- Data
- Communications

We will discuss these aspects and the resulting framework in more detail in Chapter 4. My objective is to take a look at all business aspects, both from a strategic and a tactical perspective. Then, I want to provide you, the reader, with function-specific and cross-functional concepts and tools that will help you and your business to be more successful.

In a second step, I looked through numerous lists of 'best business books of all times.' I quickly identified a list of about 60 'classics' — some older, some more recent — that are represented on most of these lists (you can also find these titles in the *References* section at the end of this book). When reading through these most influential business books of the past 100 years, I quickly found that most of these concepts and tools — many of which you will be familiar with — are:

- Still as valid today as they were 10, 20, or 50 years ago

- Easy to grasp and can be explained in relatively few words

These findings also confirmed my personal belief that there is not much need for new concepts and tools that go beyond these fundamentals (although we are all overwhelmed continuously by 'fancy new concepts and tools' — think 'old wine in new bottles').

Of course, you may need to apply completely new techniques as technologies evolve. For example, the (physical) mass mailings of the past have now been replaced by mass emails and targeted online banner ads. But, mainly, you still want to create *sales leads* and, hence, the notion of a *sales funnel* remains as relevant as ever.

Bottom line: to leverage the power of *Simplicity*, you will need to remind yourself of the fundamental concepts and tools that you are already aware of. These will suffice to tackle most of your current business challenges and build your success.

When browsing through the 'classics, ' I also noticed something that surprised me quite a bit: in most of these books, you find only a few, if any, visual representations of the essential concepts and tools. Since the 'classics' are rather 'stingy' when it comes to graphics and images, I will try to leverage the simple wisdom that "A *picture is worth a thousand words.*" This should make grasping key concepts and tools much simpler — and even fun.

As I started to write this book, I also realized that trying to write one comprehensive volume on all-things *Simplicity* would not make sense. The result would have been a too lengthy volume. Since the objective is to keep things simple, I decided to make the book you hold in your hands — 'Essentials' — the first volume of a series on *Simplicity for Success*. This way, every book of the series can focus on a specific topic shortly and crisply, keeping it simple for you — the reader.

Throughout this book, I will also highlight *Simplicity Tips* and *Simplicity Facts*. A compilation of all *Tips* and *Facts* can be found at the end of this book.

SIMPLICITY

TIP #1

A PICTURE IS WORTH A THOUSAND WORDS, SO USE IMAGES, GRAPHS, AND CHARTS A LOT.

Let's start with a heads up. As you will also find, the power of *Simplicity* comes with one caveat: making things simple is hard work! Paraphrasing Albert Einstein, one could say: "*Simplicity is 1% talent and 99% hard work*" — our Simplicity Fact #1. But that is also a good thing: you really don't have to be a genius to figure out how to leverage the power of *Simplicity*.

SIMPLICITY

FACT #1

SIMPLICITY IS 1% TALENT AND 99% HARD WORK.

Before I wrap up this introduction, a few words of both caution and encouragement: you may be tempted to dismiss some of the concepts and tools in the following chapters as trivial. Don't! Should that happen, remind yourself that by focusing on the fundamentals, you are standing on the shoulders of giants. Let your own *Common Sense* convince you of the validity of the fundamentals. This will help you to convince yourself of the power of *Simplicity*.

As you begin to apply these simple, fundamental concepts in your business, and as you are trying to convince your colleagues and team members of their power, you may encounter resistance. You may hear:

- *"You're too simplistic."*, i.e., you may be accused of oversimplifying and that a more 'ingenious' concept is needed.
- *"You don't understand."*, i.e., you may be told that the challenge at hand requires a more sophisticated solution and that you just don't understand all the nuances. Along these lines, you may also be criticized for not having conducted detailed-enough analyses.
- *"We know all that."*, i.e., your simple answers may be declared too obvious and basic.

Don't worry and stand your ground: your best revenge over your critics will be that you are right. The following chapters will provide you with an introduction to some of the critical tools of *Simplicity*. Applying these will allow you to leverage the power of *Simplicity* for your success — enjoy!

CHAPTER 2

SIMPLE IS HARD, BUT POWERFUL!

"THAT'S BEEN ONE OF MY MANTRAS —
FOCUS AND SIMPLICITY. SIMPLE CAN BE HARDER
THAN COMPLEX: YOU NEED TO WORK HARD TO
GET YOUR THINKING CLEAN TO MAKE IT SIMPLE.
BUT IT'S WORTH IT IN THE END BECAUSE ONCE
YOU GET THERE, YOU CAN MOVE MOUNTAINS."

— STEVE JOBS

We all prefer it simple. When you buy a new cell phone, car, or any other device, you want to be able to use it from the get-go, without having to read through a lengthy manual. When you're using a service or buying a product online, you want this to require only a few mouse-clicks. And at work, you want any guidance given to you by your boss and any input provided to you by your colleagues to be crystal clear. Similarly, you want any process or workflow — and any associated user interface (UX) — to be intuitive. In fact, whether at home or at work, you want any device, process, or UX to be as simple as possible.

People of all ages, religions, cultures, and political beliefs prefer *Simplicity*. In fact, this preference is burned into the basic wiring of all living cells. The fundamental processes of life and the Universe can usually be described in quite simple terms.

Think Isaac Newton: he described the essence of the (non-trivial) concept of gravitational force by using the example of an apple falling from a tree. Or think Albert Einstein: he managed to package many of the complexities of our Universe into a simple formula: $E = mc^2$.

Simplicity is elusive, though. Over time, everything in nature tends to become more disordered, less structured, and hence, less simple. In physics, this phenomenon is described in the 2nd Law of Thermodynamics.

But you don't need to be a physicist to figure this out. You have observed this fact since you were a child, probably without giving it too much thought. For example, when my son was very young, he sometimes proudly announced, "*I'm making a mess*." And he had a big smile in his face after having scattered his toys all around the living room. We all know that 'fixing a mess', i.e., putting things back into their place, giving things structure, making things simpler again, takes much more effort than 'making a mess'.

SIMPLICITY
FACT #2

SIMPLICITY IS ELUSIVE. OVER TIME, EVERYTHING IN NATURE TENDS TO BECOME MORE DISORDERED, LESS STRUCTURED, AND HENCE, LESS SIMPLE.

In the world at large, as in any business, most things are not naturally simple. You need to make (and keep) them simple, which is a constant uphill battle. That's *The Paradox of Simplicity*: Simple is hard!

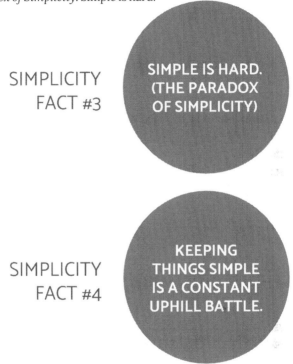

SIMPLICITY
FACT #3

SIMPLE IS HARD.
(THE PARADOX
OF SIMPLICITY)

SIMPLICITY
FACT #4

KEEPING
THINGS SIMPLE
IS A CONSTANT
UPHILL BATTLE.

Simplicity:
The Love Child of Brains and Common Sense

Let's start our journey on *Simplicity for Success* by defining *Simplicity*. One standard definition for *Simplicity* is "*the quality or condition of being easy to understand or do.*" Great: so simple is "*easy-to-understand-or-do*" and that's certainly what we all prefer over "*difficult-to-understand-or-do.*"

You have achieved *Simplicity* when you hear your colleagues, customers, or users say things like:

- *"I fully understand why we are making this decision and what the next steps are."*
- *"This user interface is absolutely intuitive and easy to use."*
- *"This product has everything I need and nothing more."*

Simplicity, when achieved, can make you more successful since, for example:

- Decisions that are easy to understand and have clearly defined next steps are much more likely to get implemented.
- Users of software applications are much less likely to make mistakes or add the wrong information if the user interface and process are simple and straightforward.
- Customers are more likely to buy a product if it gets them just what they need, and they immediately understand how to use it.

Given that the average person has an IQ of around 100, it is safe to assume that anyone who reads these lines fulfills a fundamental prerequisite for being able to leverage *Simplicity* for success: you've got the necessary brains!

All we need to add to this fact is a healthy dose of *Common Sense.* One standard definition for *Common Sense* is *"good sense and sound judgment in practical matters"* — which I am sure you have as well.

Bottom line: you don't need to be a genius. If you are (unexceptionally) smart and practical, you will be able to leverage *Simplicity* for success. This book, and the other books of the series, will explain how.

Still not convinced? Ok, then let's look at a more complicated definition of *Common Sense*: "*good judgment or prudence in estimating or managing affairs, free from emotional bias or intellectual subtlety and not dependent on special or technical knowledge*." Phew — what a mouthful. But look at the last part: "*not dependent on special or technical knowledge*."

In other words: don't be afraid if you are not an expert on a specific topic; trust your *Common Sense*! When applying *Common Sense*, you should use cold logic, while eliminating both sentiment and self-interest from your judgment.

Renaissance genius Leonardo da Vinci had an interesting perspective on *Common Sense*. He saw the human mind as a laboratory for gathering material from eyes, ears, and other organs of perception — material that was then channeled through the 'organ of common sense.' In da Vinci's view, *Common Sense* is a sort of 'super-sense' that coordinates and analyses all the other senses. The man was a genius, so let's trust his perspective.

If you prefer a more recent perspective, look at this statement by management professor Henry Mintzberg:

> "*Management is a curious phenomenon: it's generously paid, enormously influential, and significantly devoid of common sense.*"

According to Mintzberg's observations, many people in today's business world refuse to trust da Vinci's 'super-sense' or rather: their own *Common Sense*.

Ken Segall, author of *Insanely Simple: The Obsession That Drives Apple's Success*, in which he describes working closely with the late Steve Jobs, also supports this notion:

> *"Simplicity isn't afraid to act on common sense,*
> *even when it runs counter to an expert's opinion."*

My personal observations over the past decades have been similar. In fact, one could occasionally get the impression that some people leave their *Common Sense* in the parking lot when they come to work. So be more trusting in your own capabilities, your instincts, your intuition, your *Common Sense*.

SIMPLICITY

TIP #2

IN YOUR QUEST TO LEVERAGE SIMPLICITY FOR SUCCESS, MAKE AMPLE USE OF YOUR COMMON SENSE.

The only disclaimer in this regard is probably that your confidence in yourself will grow over time. That's something I have experienced myself. When I was still relatively new to the profession of management consulting, I remember walking down a long hallway at a globally leading car manufacturer with one of my partners. We discussed a client-related matter, and the partner said: *"Trust your gut: when something seems fishy, it probably is – this is common sense."* I looked at the partner and said: *"I know what you mean. This may be common sense, but with my limited experience, I'm hesitant to trust my gut just yet."*

Over time I learned to 'trust my gut' and rely on my *Common Sense* – you can do the same, and I assure you that your confidence will increase over time.

This introductory verbiage may sound too good to be true. But I am sure that this book will both convince you and provide you with the necessary self-confidence. You will be able to leverage the power of *Simplicity* by using your brains and your *Common Sense*.

Simplicity and its 'Evil Twin': Complexity

Above, I have mentioned that Albert Einstein managed to package many of the complexities of our Universe into a simple formula: $E = mc^2$. Of course, if you were trying to dig deeper into the implications of Einstein's famous formula, it would get as fascinating as it would get mind boggling. But do you need to understand all the details of how the Universe is behaving to be sure that the Sun will rise tomorrow morning again? No, you don't!

Similarly, with ½ a gallon of water and around 2,000 kcal of nutritious food per day, your body is usually able to make it through the day. Simple. Typically, you don't spend much time thinking about the specifics of your bodily functions and how they enable you to breathe, digest, walk, and work. Trying to understand the details of your bodily functions, how your food and drink help the functioning of every single cell in your body would get incredibly complex. Do you need this level of understanding to make it through the day? No, you don't!

At this point, meet the evil twin of *Simplicity*: *Complexity*.

SIMPLICITY
FACT #5

COMPLEXITY
IS THE 'EVIL TWIN'
OF SIMPLICITY.

Whether you are thinking about your bodily processes, the mechanics of our solar system, or your business challenges and opportunities – always focus on what is relevant. In other words: you need to simplify the challenge at hand such that you can comfortably understand, explain, and manage it.

By doing so, you will fight the 'evil twin' *Complexity* every step of the way. If you don't do this, you can easily be overwhelmed by complexities. In real business life, *Complexity* creeping in typically results in endless and pointless meetings, unnecessary consumption of resources, and limited tangible outcomes. Sound familiar?

Based on my experience, the three key indicators of *Complexity* at work are typically:

1. Lack of clear goals and objectives
2. Ineffective communication
3. Lack of competence

Especially in complex, changing environments, it is essential to have clear goals and objectives, with all key stakeholders in alignment.

Simple, crystal-clear communication – targeting for decision-making and concrete action – is the linchpin toward achieving these clear goals and objectives.

SIMPLICITY

FACT #6

THE THREE KEY INDICATORS OF COMPLEXITY ARE:
1. LACK OF CLEAR GOALS AND OBJECTIVES
2. INEFFECTIVE COMMUNICATION
3. LACK OF COMPETENCE

But *Complexity* is often also used as an excuse to cover up shortcomings, performance issues, or simply incompetence.

It isn't always possible to convince colleagues, bosses, or clients to apply relatively simple solutions or performance levers to achieve substantial improvements.

Once I was trying to highlight to the leadership of a client how a relatively simple tool (*sales funnel tracking*) would lead to increased transparency on sales performance. This would open the door to substantial improvements in sales performance management and, ultimately, sales. The leader of the sales operations team told me, "*Well, you don't have much experience in sales, have you? Our sales processes are highly complex. I don't have the time to explain all of these complicated aspects to you.*"

As I later learned, this sales operations leader also went behind my back and shared her perspectives on my (in)competence with company leadership. Well, I did have more sales experience than this person was aware of. Also, the situation was not all that complicated. In fact, this person did not want to explain the (far-from-complex) specifics of sales operations to me. This would have made painfully obvious that this person was not only incompetent, but also a weak leader and, hence, responsible for severe shortcomings in the sales organization. Indirectly, I had already figured this out.

Fortunately, I had a solid trust-based relationship with the company's CEO, and the sales leadership team soon saw some changes on the personnel front.

Lesson learned: often, it is not enough to be right about something. You also need to develop trust-based relationships with key stakeholders to be heard. But that's a topic for a very different book.

In terms of *Complexity* drivers, we can look at five key areas that describe the operations of any business:

1. *Processes*, i.e., the design of any business process.
2. *Products/Services*, especially their design and variety.
3. *Communications*, i.e., both written and oral (esp. presentations).
4. *Organization*, e.g., structure and performance management.
5. *Strategy*, especially the associated analyses and decision-making.

These five key areas are all interrelated, as shown in the graphic below. The challenge is to first drive everything related to these key areas from *Complexity* toward *Simplicity*, and then keep things simple.

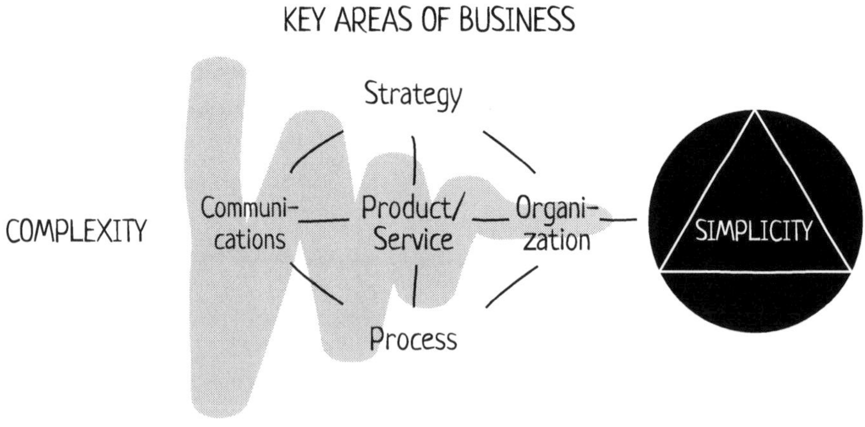

KEY AREAS OF BUSINESS

FIGURE 1

COMPLEXITY AND KEY AREAS OF BUSINESS

You will probably have come across numerous real-life examples of *Complexity* related to the above five key areas. Moving toward the right, i.e., in the direction of *Simplicity*, is typically hard work. This is true both for every single area, as well as for the overall system.

So please make a mental note on your overall key objective that this book, and the book series, will help you to:

> *Eliminate Complexity, foster Simplicity*
> *along all key areas of your business.*

In this regard, on your journey toward Simplicity for success, you should keep one additional fact in mind:

> *Success is about doing the right thing,*
> *not about doing everything right.*

We will jointly explore practical examples of this notion, which drives us toward the need for prioritization.

SIMPLICITY
FACT #7

SUCCESS
IS ABOUT DOING
THE RIGHT THING,
NOT ABOUT DOING
EVERYTHING RIGHT.

CHAPTER 3

MASTERS OF SIMPLICITY

"REAL SIMPLICITY MEANS THAT
WHICH GIVES THE VERY BEST SERVICE
AND IS THE MOST CONVENIENT IN USE."

— HENRY FORD

Simplicity leads to extraordinary success, as borne out by many case studies on the Masters of *Simplicity* of the past 100 years. In fact, many of the companies founded by great *Simplifiers* are household names. They include Henry Ford, the McDonald's Brothers & Ray Kroc, Walt Disney, Ingvar Kamprad, Steve Jobs, James Dyson, Jeff Bezos, Larry Page & Sergey Brin, to name just a few.

These entrepreneurs have built businesses based on offering easy-to-understand products or services. And all of them pushed for *Simplicity*. Some of them made that quite plain. For example, Henry Ford said of his revolutionary new car, the Model T, "*Its most important feature is its simplicity.*" Ray Kroc, who built the McDonald's chain into the empire that it is today, said, "*My first motto was KISS: Keep It Simple, Stupid.*"

Let's look more closely at the examples of Apple, Amazon, McDonalds, and Starbucks and how they leverage Simplicity for success. Few readers will be current or former employees of any of these companies, so you will not be familiar with their inner workings.

I am sure, however, that most of you are customers or users of the products or services of these companies. This means that you literally have a 'personal' relationship with these companies and can relate to their products, services, and processes. So please keep your own experiences in mind as you read through the following examples.

Apple

Apple is probably the leading Master of Simplicity. Look at their products: simple, intuitive designs make them easy to use, and the available product range is minimal. Look at their branding: simple and clean. Look at their stores: the same minimalist design the world over, with someone waiting for you at the entrance who asks you for your need, adds you to the (virtual) line, or points you in the right direction.

To quote Ken Segall, who has worked closely with the late Steve Jobs and who has written extensively about his experiences at Apple, "*What sets Apple apart and what makes Apple stand out in a complicated world: a deep, almost religious belief in the power of simplicity. Apple's focus on simplicity is unique. It goes beyond enthusiasm, beyond passion, all the way to obsession. There's nothing subtle about Apple's love affair with simplicity. It's everywhere you look. It's in the company's products, its ads, its internal organization, its stores, and its customer relationships. Inside Apple, simplicity is a goal, a work style, a measuring stick, a common thread that ties everything together.*"

This 'obsession' has made Apple one of the most valuable companies on Earth.

SIMPLICITY

TIP #3

MAKE SIMPLICITY AN 'OBSESSION'.

Amazon

When was the last time you ordered from Amazon? Probably days ago, rather than weeks. And possibly, like me, you started ordering from them in the late 1990's when all they offered was books. Fast forward 20 years, and the range of products you can order from *Amazon* is now almost unlimited: from books to clothes and hardware all the way to groceries.

Amazon has become a vast global marketplace. Yet the ordering process itself hasn't changed much — easy as 1-2-3, and you can even set-up a '1-click order'. Spectacularly simple.

Amazon are also the masters of *personalized marketing*: did you buy a book? Well, you will soon receive an email (or see a banner ad online somewhere) that suggests another book, that is somehow related to your purchase. You need a reminder on a refill of, say, diapers — Amazon will remind you.

The 'back-end engine' that enables this *personalized marketing* is sophisticated and 'AI-driven,' i.e., based on artificial intelligence, but that is none of your concern. It has been developed to make your life simpler (and, of course, to make Amazon's revenues grow further). Yet, you never get to 'see' its complexity.

Bottom line: Amazon keeps it simple for you (at the user interface or 'front-end'), while mastering complexities at the 'back-end' that are 'invisible' to you as a customer.

It is safe to say that no one has mastered this combination of *Simplicity* on the 'front-end' based on some serious *Complexity* on the 'back-end' like Amazon has. As a result, Amazon has become one of the most valuable companies on Earth.

McDonald's & Starbucks

But it's not only in the online space that we find masters of *Simplicity*. Irrespectively of whether you are a fan of McDonald's food or whether you like Starbuck's coffee, I am sure that you have been inside a restaurant of both chains. What do they have in common? Everything is standardized and, hence, simple.

Today, McDonald's operates over 35,000 restaurants in more than 100 countries, while Starbucks operates over 25,000 locations in more than 60 countries. Except for some local specifics in terms of product offerings and design, the way you buy your Big Mac or Grande Latte is pretty much the same everywhere. You order your (customized) food and drink, pay, wait a few minutes to get your order prepared, then grab it from the pick-up counter.

To make things even simpler, you can now (pre-)order using an app or a self-order screen in-store. Simple and easy for you because it works the same way everywhere. Successful for both McDonald's and Starbucks since they are the globally largest restaurant and coffee house chains, respectively.

One interesting fact that you may not be aware of is that the *Simplicity* journey toward success was quite a long one for both McDonald's and Starbucks. The McDonald's brothers opened their first restaurant in 1940 in San Bernardino, CA. In 1955, Ray Kroc franchised the 9th McDonald's restaurant. In 1961 he bought all of the little over 100 restaurants from the McDonald's brothers.

The first Starbucks opened in Seattle in 1971. In 1987, the original owners sold Starbucks to Howard Schultz, and only then locations outside Seattle were opened. At the IPO in 1992, Starbucks had 110 locations. In both cases, it took about 20 years from the first to the 100th location and, in both cases, the rest is history.

If *Simplicity* is so powerful, why on Earth aren't other companies simply copying the methods applied by Apple, Amazon, McDonald's, and Starbucks to achieve the same level of success?

The short answer: It ain't easy. Or, in other words, the success stories of the Masters of *Simplicity* are proving the point that simple is hard.

What's more: making *Simplicity* part of the DNA of a start-up is one thing. The changes required to embed the principles of *Simplicity* at an existing, possibly long-established business are a whole different challenge. Being serious about *Simplicity* at an established business typically involves a lot of change — which, in turn, tends to create a lot of resistance. This means that every ambassador of *Simplicity* needs to be prepared for an uphill battle.

But in both cases, it is a worthwhile effort. Embedding *Simplicity* often requires more time, more energy, and maybe even, initially, more money. It might require you to step on a few toes. But more times than not, it will lead to measurably better results and success for the business.

LEVERAGING
THE POWER OF SIMPLICITY

CHAPTER 4

THE POWER
OF SIMPLICITY:
ESSENTIALS

"I APOLOGIZE FOR SUCH A LONG LETTER—
I DIDN'T HAVE TIME TO WRITE A SHORT ONE."

— MARK TWAIN

n the following, you will learn about the How to leverage the power of Simplicity. One thing that you need to keep in mind on the journey upon which we are going to embark together is: you can do it!

Let's start with a few simple, very fundamental business principles which tell the story of virtually every company:

- The principal objective of a business is to maximize *Profit*.
- Given that *Profit* equals *Revenue* minus *Cost* ...
- ... you want to maximize your *Revenue* ...
- ... while minimizing your *Cost*.

- On the *Revenue* side, you need to keep in mind that *Customers* love simple, easy-to-use products, services, and processes.
- On the *Cost* side, you need to keep in mind that your *Employees* love clarity, simple processes, and recognition.
- Hence, you need to put systems and processes in place that are making both your *Customers* and *Employees* happy.

Common sense, right? To ensure your success, you might want to add three considerations that should help you to indeed follow the path of *Simplicity* and *common sense*:

- Always leave your ego out of the situation.
- Avoid wishful thinking.
- Be better at listening — *common sense* is often based on what others know.

SIMPLICITY
FACT #8

THE SIMPLE EQUATION
DRIVING EVERY BUSINESS IS:
PROFIT = REVENUE – COST;
YOU WANT TO
MAXIMIZE REVENUE
AND MINIMIZE COST.

We human beings are pre-disposed toward *Simplicity*, so every one of us can tap into its power. Simple concepts and tools usually have a ring of truth about them. You may distrust your instincts and feel there must be a hidden, more complicated answer. Don't!

What's evident to you is evident to many. That's why *Simplicity* has so much power. When you simplify complex issues, you will be able to define processes that have just the right level of detail. You will design analyses that address the core challenge at hand, and you will facilitate fact-based decisions that don't require too much debate.

But as I had indicated earlier: expect to encounter skeptics. When you embark on your first 'crusades' as an advocate of *Simplicity*, you may be faced with resistance. The disciples of *Complexity* will inevitably argue that something cannot be done or that your suggestion is simplistic. Don't get discouraged! Push!

And please take special note of the quote by Steve Jobs at the beginning of Chapter 2: "*Simple can be harder than complex: you have to work hard to get your thinking clean to make it simple.*" This reiterates the *Paradox of Simplicity* that I had introduced earlier. But there is the bright side that you need to keep in mind:

Simple is hard but powerful!

Let's start to talk about tools. The most universal tool of *Simplicity* is what I call the *Virtuous Cycle of Simplicity*: Structure — Prioritize — Iterate. In other words, the *Virtuous Cycle of Simplicity* helps you to focus. In turn, focus helps you to achieve *Simplicity*. No matter what problem you are trying to solve, you first need to create some structure. Once the structure is in place, you need to prioritize. And then, in most cases, you will need to iterate. This is where simple often becomes hard, since you may have to iterate quite a few times until you have found the right structure and identified the right priorities.

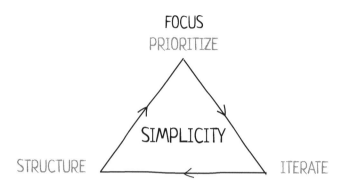

FIGURE 2

THE VIRTUOUS CYCLE OF SIMPLICITY:
STRUCTURE – PRIORITIZE – ITERATE

SIMPLICITY
FACT #9

THE VIRTUOUS
CYCLE OF SIMPLICITY:
STRUCTURE –
PRIORITIZE – ITERATE.

SIMPLICITY
FACT #10

SIMPLICITY HELPS YOU
TO FOCUS;
FOCUS HELPS YOU
TO ACHIEVE SIMPLICITY.

The *Virtuous Cycle of Simplicity* is a universal tool you can apply for every type of problem-solving. We will discuss problem-solving in Chapters 6 through 9. Let's first look at the universe of potential problems to be solved. In the below *Framework of Simplicity Tools*, you find 3 vertical segments:

* Data
* Planning — Products & Services — People ('3Ps')
* Communications

On top of these 3 vertical segments, you find a horizontal bar: *Essentials*. This bar represents the contents of this book with its three sections:

* Understanding the power of *Simplicity*
* Leveraging the power of *Simplicity*
* *Problem Solving* — The *Magic Tool of Simplicity*

In other words: the *Essentials* are also relevant for every type of problem to be solved, especially the problem-solving process that we will discuss in Chapters 6 through 9.

Under the '3Ps' in the center of the *Framework*, you find all key business functions. These functions can be found across all industries and at all types of businesses — from start-ups to major corporations. Specifically, under *Planning*, you find:

* *Strategy & Planning*
* *Finance & Budgeting*
* *Concept & Tools* (that are relevant for planning across functions)

Under *Products & Services*, you find:

- *Design & Development*
- *Marketing & Sales*
- *Procurement & Negotiation*

Finally, under *People* you find:

- *Recruitment & Performance Management*
- *Operations*
- *Customer Relations*

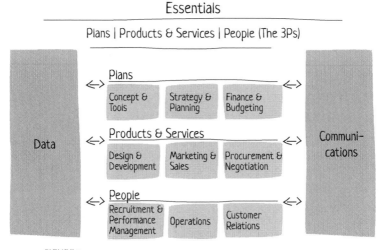

FIGURE 3
FRAMEWORK OF SIMPLICITY TOOLS

The two segments to the left and right — *Data* and *Communications* — are relevant across all business functions:

- As we will discuss in the next chapter, *Data* is of continuously increasing importance for all businesses. Hence, it is crucial to apply the concepts and tools of *Simplicity* in data analyses and digital transformations. Primarily, it is essential to understand if and how the application of advanced tools such as Artificial Intelligence (AI) can be leveraged for business success.

- *Simplicity* in *Communications* can be hugely beneficial for any business and across business functions. In that sense, Chapter 9 provides an overview of how *top-down* storytelling can vastly improve the decision-making process. Besides, applying the concepts and tools of *Simplicity* can help to plan and execute much more efficient — and successful — meetings and workshops.

Ultimately, the topics mentioned above will all be covered in detail in the *Simplicity for Success* series (specifics in this regard at the end of this book).

Simplicity and its Powerful Ally: Standardization

Common sense will tell you that *standardization* is a helpful ally of *Simplicity*. Only recently, I worked for one of the leading computer storage device manufacturers. There, the inputs from different product marketing team members to the engineering team all looked different. Some sent slides, some sent a spreadsheet, some sent both. The order of categories of required specifications and features mostly differed. When I realized that, I suggested a standardized template or at least a standardized structure. Specifically, the most important specifications and features should be at the top, followed by specifications and features sorted by category in a pre-defined order. Everybody was happy, since *standardization* made life easier for both product marketers and engineers. *Simplicity* in action.

I am sure you could come up with many similar examples, both from your personal and professional life. When you come across such an instance, often all you need to do is to ask whether it might be possible to simplify or standardize a specific input or process. Chances are that you may find a lot of appreciation for such a suggestion. However, you may also have to overcome some resistance. It's human nature that we are often afraid of any kind of change, even it is for our own good.

SIMPLICITY

TIP #4

SIMPLIFY BY STANDARDIZING WHEREVER YOU CAN – YOUR COLLEAGUES AND CUSTOMERS WILL LOVE YOU FOR IT!

In the next chapter, let's look at why *Simplicity* is of increasing importance in today's age of *Big Data*, *Data Lakes*, *Data Science*, and *Artificial Intelligence (AI)*. *We will* then focus on the *Magic Tool of Simplicity: Problem-solving*.

CHAPTER 5

THE FOUNDATION
OF SIMPLICITY: DATA

"THE GOAL IS TO TURN DATA INTO INFORMATION
AND INFORMATION INTO INSIGHT."

— CARLY FIORINA

Situation:
Exponential Increase in Data and Information

We live in a world that is becoming increasingly interconnected and amassing ever-increasing amounts of data and information. It's all about the internet, and you keep hearing the term *Big Data*. This is wonderful in many ways: when traveling, you can easily chat online with your loved ones at home. And if you are looking for specific types of information, you can usually find them somewhere on the internet with just a few clicks.

Can we quantify the notion of 'ever increasing amounts of data and information'? Legendary architect and inventor Buckminster 'Bucky' Fuller — best known for coining the phrase *Spaceship Earth* — defined what is known as the *Knowledge Doubling Curve*. He noted that as of the year 1900, human knowledge doubled approximately every century. By the end of World War II, knowledge was doubling every 25 years.

Today things are not as simple, because different types of knowledge have different rates of growth. But on average, human knowledge is supposedly doubling about once every year. According to IBM, the build-out of the *Internet of Things (IoT)* will lead to the doubling of knowledge every 12 hours.

Currently, humankind is probably creating a few EB or Exabytes of information per year. To put this number into perspective: a single novel is equivalent to about 1 MB (Megabyte), so we are creating the equivalent of billions and billions of novels in information per year. It is probably fair to argue that the majority of these EBs is 'data' rather than 'knowledge.' However, distilling 'knowledge' from 'data' is a challenge that is one of the keys to leveraging *Simplicity* for success.

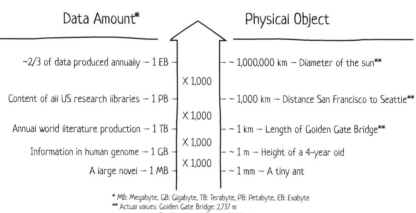

FIGURE 4

DATA AMOUNTS COMPARED TO PHYSICAL OBJECTS

The exponential increase in data availability also drives the need for ever more specialization and specific expertise everywhere in business, engineering, and science. For example, the relatively new fields of *Data Science* and *Artificial Intelligence* (AI) have become the latest trends, especially in the worlds of science, business, and education.

While more and more companies hire their own teams of data scientists, there is to date not even a clear definition of the term *Data Science*. Mostly, it's about using all sorts of tools, such as algorithms and statistical methods to derive relevant insights from the ever-increasing oceans of data that exist inside companies.

Both the wealth of data and the new tools open the doors to new, exciting opportunities across all functions of a business. Properly utilized, data, along with the methods of *Data Science* and AI, can help to increase customer value and revenue, as well as customer satisfaction and process efficiencies, while reducing cost.

The promise looms large, yet most people currently fall into one of two camps when it comes to all these new tools and possibilities:

- The *Enthusiasts*: they get somewhat carried away and assume that *Data Science* and AI can provide solutions to all their business challenges.
- The *Overwhelmed*: they see all these new tools, yet do not know what exactly to do with them and how to leverage the related promises and possibilities.

As for the *Enthusiasts*: I have indeed come across numerous success stories. I found these not only at high-tech companies like Amazon or Google, but also across various other industries, ranging from insurance via health care all the way to oil & gas. The *Key Factors of Success* (KFS) that are the prerequisite for any successful *Data Science*- or AI-based project were always the same across industries:

- Leadership backing and involvement
- Clearly defined business objectives and outcomes
- Stakeholder buy-in across functions

These KFS sound simple enough. Yet, I have come across many more cases where these prerequisites were not in place, and many resources were wasted or (sometimes false) hopes disappointed.

The *Overwhelmed* typically do not know where to start. They hear about all these new possibilities and feel that they somehow need to keep up with the competition. As a result, the default reaction is then often to install a team of data scientists (frequently without a clear objective) or hire a Chief Data Officer. This may very well be the right choice, but only if the KFS mentioned above are applied religiously.

Complication:
Too much Data, too many Choices ...

That said, let's step back for a minute and shed some light on what *Big Data* and *Data Science* are all about. I have strong evidence that many business professionals — even in Silicon Valley, where I am based — do not really understand this. Let's try to de-mystify these two terms by first looking at their definitions.

Generally, *Big Data* is a term that simply describes a large, potentially complex set of data. The promise of *Big Data* is that analyses of large data sets can find new data correlations. These can help to identify business trends or customer interests, but also to prevent diseases or combat crime. The place where all the data of a business is stored is often called a *Data Lake*.

Along these lines, *Data Science* employs techniques and theories drawn from statistics, as well as information and computer sciences, to detect the correlations mentioned above. In other words, *Data Science* is nothing but a fancier term for what could also be called 'advanced statistics.'

Increasing interconnectedness and almost limitless access to data and information are also driving *Complexity* on many levels. In particular, you are facing the challenge of having to use, analyze, and digest the increasing amounts of data using new concepts, frameworks, methods, and software tools at work and in your daily life.

The possibilities of harnessing the power of data (think: dashboards), *Data Science* (think: online lead generation), and AI (think: self-driving cars) are huge. But, as indicated, to leverage these, you need, for starters, to have clearly defined objectives in place.

The most significant risk we are running is, generally, that we end up not seeing the forest for the trees. Along these lines, when dealing with data, always keep in mind one of the fundamental laws of computer science:

Garbage in,
garbage out!

SIMPLICITY
TIP #5

**IN DATA ANALYSES,
ALWAYS KEEP THIS LAW
OF COMPUTER SCIENCE
IN MIND:
GARBAGE IN,
GARBAGE OUT!**

In other words: using the wrong data or a faulty algorithm will result in incorrect output data. But the output data will not tell you if it is wrong. Hence, it is essential that you:

- Ask the right question(s)
- Ensure that you use the right data
- Have at least a high-level understanding of what the algorithm or tool is doing

Sounds simple? I can't even begin to count the number of situations I have experienced where this simple approach was not followed properly.

A classic case in terms of 'asking the right questions' is the definition of a management dashboard. Today, there are myriads of *Management Information Systems* (MIS) that you can plug on top of your business data. These allow you to create dashboards of all shapes and sizes.

I have experienced situations where the task of defining and implementing an MIS was given to the IT Team. The problem: while the IT Team will ensure that the right data will be accessed and presented, the real 'heavy lifting' lies in the creation of an 'insightful' management dashboard.

Designing a 'crisp' dashboard that captures the most critical business metrics or *Key Performance*

Indicators (KPIs) is, in fact, both an art and hard work. Yet often not enough time and thought is spent on identifying a minimal set of the most critical KPIs.

One possible result that I have experienced: every Monday morning, the entire executive leadership team of a client spent an hour discussing a dashboard of about 70(!) KPIs. Trust me: not all KPIs were equally important, and on many Monday mornings, top management did not discuss the most pressing challenges at hand. (For those of you who do not have much experience with executive dashboards: they should typically consist of no more than 10-20 KPIs — ideally fewer; the fewer, the better.)

How can you deal with the challenges of data 'overload' and *Complexity*, as well as the resulting myriad of tool choices? The simple answer: *Simplicity* and focus.

Solution: Simplicity and Focus

Simplicity can help you to focus, i.e., to structure and prioritize (see Chapter 4). As a result, you will conduct the most relevant analyses and make the most impactful decisions, even as the size of your *Data Lake* is increasing.

To re-iterate: more data does not necessarily result in more relevant insights. Instead, you need to ask the right questions and conduct the right analyses. To define these, you do not have to be a data scientist yourself. However, you need to apply business (common) sense. And you have to be able to guide your analysts and data scientists. They need to conduct the analyses and develop the tools that truly impact the top line and/or the bottom line of your business. To do that, you can rely on your two new best friends: *Simplicity* and *common sense*.

SIMPLICITY
FACT #11

MORE DATA DOES NOT NECESSARILY RESULT IN MORE RELEVANT INSIGHTS.

As more and more data become available, and decisions seem to be even harder to make, the ability to leverage *Simplicity* becomes more valuable. In general, to harness the power of your data and data analytics, you should follow this 6-step approach:

1. Identify (and prioritize) the challenge(s) you want to solve.
2. Define your target objective(s) and the associated key drivers.
3. Create transparency on the available data.
4. Identify tools/techniques that may help you achieve your objectives.
5. Develop a pilot set-up (aka *sandbox*) to verify feasibility.
6. Implement the tools/process and roll-out across the organization.

The business challenge can be anything from reducing cost to increasing customer satisfaction. No matter what the challenge, you always need to identify the key drivers of, e.g., cost, customer satisfaction, or process efficiency.

This approach is also another lesson on *simple is hard*. While the above 6-step process itself is simple and straightforward, there are numerous hurdles you need to overcome as you move from idea to implementation. We will discuss these in more detail in a future volume of the series.

Still, adhering to this simple process is your guarantee that you can leverage the power of *Simplicity* as related to data and analytics. Or, in case you run into some showstoppers, 'abandon mission' early and save a lot of money.

Keep in mind that all the new tools and techniques are simply a means to an end. They may have a powerful, positive impact on your results, if properly utilized — or they may be the proverbial sledgehammer that you're using to crack a nut. In other words: in many cases, you will find that *AI*, *Big Data*, and *Data Science* are <u>not</u> the appropriate answer to your challenges. There may be much simpler approaches and tools that can help you to achieve the desired outcomes.

More important than any tools and techniques is that you clearly explain to your managers, vendors, analysts, data engineers, or data scientists the business challenge you need to get solved. Once you have provided a clearly defined objective, you can ask them to come back with potential solutions.

Ideally, they should also come back with some sort of cost-benefit or *Return-of-Investment (ROI)* calculation. If a complex technical project involving a lot of data science and computing power results in an ROI of 150% — great. But maybe a simple training program for your sales team can have the same effect. That's on you to figure out.

CHAPTER 6

THE MAGIC TOOL OF SIMPLICITY: PROBLEM-SOLVING

"THE GREATEST IDEAS ARE THE SIMPLEST."

—WILLIAM GOLDING

Disclaimer: Simple, but not simplistic!

Before we continue, let me remind you that the key objective of this book is to teach you how to apply *Simplicity* for maximum impact, e.g., by increasing efficiency or effectiveness. But it is not at all about being *simplistic.*

Simplistic means oversimplified, as in *"treating complex issues and problems as if they were much simpler than they really are."* The difference between *simple* and *simplistic* is crucial. As Albert Einstein famously said:

"Make things as simple as possible,
but not simpler."

Identifying the fine line between *simple* and *simplistic* is undoubtedly not easy. The distinction between the two lies in the ability to understand what is essential and meaningful as opposed to what is not, e. g., to a product, service, or process. You then need to ruthlessly eliminate what is not essential and meaningful and put emphasis and focus on what is left.

The difference between *simple* and *simplistic* may be nicely explained using examples from the world of space. With SpaceX, Elon Musk made space launchers *simple*. He simplified the design, manufacturing, and operations of the vehicles. As a result, his Falcon-9 launch vehicles are much cheaper and more successful than anything the competition has to offer. An example of a *simplistic* approach is the Lunar X-Prize. It was announced in 2007 and provided a total of US$30 million in prize money. The money would be awarded to the first privately funded team to land a robot on the Moon, successfully travel on the lunar surface, and transmit back images and video. Why anyone would strive to win $30 million by first having to spend significantly over $100 million (launch, robot, and operations included) I never really understood. The competition was closed in 2018 after no one came even close to claiming the prize money.

Based on my own experience, three simple guidelines typically help you avoid falling into the *simplistic* trap:

- *Clearly define the objective* (e.g., of your product, service, analysis, or project).
- As you work toward your objective, *consider as much detail as necessary, but as little as possible.*
- *Work with a team where the members represent all relevant areas of expertise* to ensure that you have

captured all that is essential and meaningful while having eliminated the rest.

In the example of the Lunar X-Prize, the objective was clearly defined. Still, the concept of the competition was *simplistic* in that it significantly underestimated the complexities and costs associated with achieving the mission objectives. A complex challenge was treated as being much simpler than it really was.

SIMPLICITY
FACT #12

TO GET THINGS 'SIMPLE' (YET NOT 'SIMPLISTIC'), YOU NEED TO IDENTIFY WHAT IS ESSENTIAL AND MEANINGFUL AS OPPOSED TO WHAT ISN'T.

The Magic Tool of Simplicity: Problem-solving

Problem-solving is the *Magic Tool of Simplicity* because it is relevant across all business functions and for all types of problems. It is based on what we can call the *Three Pillars of Simplicity*:

1. *Problem Structuring*
2. *Analysis*
3. *Story-lining & Decision-making*

These *Pillars* are relevant and helpful, independent of the challenge you are trying to address. When you want to explain, for example, a strategic road map, a vendor selection, or an organizational change, you always need a convincing, solid story. It needs to be based on a set of options, and preceded by analyses of the properly structured problem.

Across all *Three Pillars*, you need to continuously prioritize and focus, i.e., you need to apply the *Virtuous Cycle of Simplicity* that we have discussed in Chapter 4.

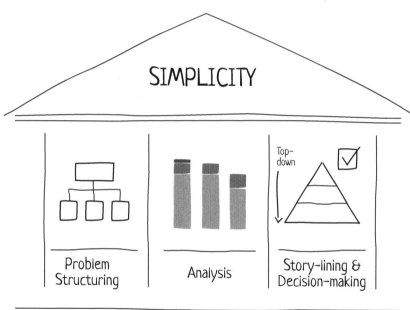

FIGURE 5

PROBLEM SOLVING: THE THREE PILLARS

I will explain the *Three Pillars* to you in the following three chapters, sharing several practical examples on how to apply these. I will also introduce a variety of tools that will help you to structure, analyze, and story-line.

Before digging into the details of structure — analyze — story-line and, ultimately, decision-making, I would like to share another simple, yet powerful consideration to keep in mind:

> *Doing the most important thing*
> *is always the most important thing.*

This is a kind of shortcut toward decision-making that is based on *common sense*. In other words: once you have figured out your most important thing — start executing. You may potentially continue to analyze, focus, and iterate as required. But it's critical that you get going, since time is, in most cases, of the essence.

SIMPLICITY
TIP #6

SIMPLY DOING THE MOST IMPORTANT THING IS ALWAYS THE MOST IMPORTANT THING.

PROBLEM-SOLVING: THE THREE PILLARS OF SIMPLICITY

CHAPTER 7

PILLAR #1:
PROBLEM STRUCTURING

"ORDER AND SIMPLIFICATION ARE THE FIRST STEPS
TOWARDS MASTERY OF A SUBJECT."

—THOMAS MANN

As we have discussed, reaching simple but powerful solutions, conclusions, and recommendations requires hard work. It starts with many hours spent on structuring problems, as well as defining and conducting analyses. Then you need to review the results of these analyses to identify the so-called *SoWhats*. Finally, story lines and recommendations have to be drafted, and presentations wordsmithed, to prepare decision-making, and, ultimately, implement solutions.

Our general education and many management trainings tend to teach us to deal with every variable, seek out every option, analyze every angle. This often leads to maddening complexity and the production of (too) many analyses and recommendations.

Simplicity requires that you structure and prioritize

from the onset – and again and again. Hence, we need to start by applying the first *Pillar of Simplicity: Problem Structuring.*

The problem-solving approach, i.e., our *Magic Tool of Simplicity*, that we will discuss in this chapter, is derived from what McKinsey calls the *hypothesis-driven approach.* This means that you need to try and 'solve' the problem before really getting to work. Remember what my Ph.D. advisor had suggested? "*Write the conclusions first.*"

This sounds highly counter-intuitive and goes against most of what we were trained to do all the way through grad school or university (especially in science or engineering).

For most of us, it's merely natural to build up to a conclusion by first reciting all the facts, then recapping all analyses, and finally reviewing all the supporting ideas. And then get to the 'punch line.' This approach is still being used very often in a business context. Yet, it is typically not very helpful, mainly because it goes against the need to prioritize and focus.

If you are puzzled and unsure, what all this means – trust me: I've been there. In principle, the approach is simple and requires you to take 3 steps:

1. Structure and review all available data and information.
2. Generate a hypothesis (if possible, a fact-based one).
3. Identify the key questions to prove or disprove your hypothesis.

SIMPLICITY

TIP #7

PROBLEM STRUCTURING NEEDS TO FOLLOW 3 STEPS:
1. STRUCTURE AND REVIEW ALL AVAILABLE DATA
2. GENERATE A FACT-BASED HYPOTHESIS
3. IDENTIFY THE KEY QUESTIONS TO PROVE OR DISPROVE YOUR HYPOTHESIS

The Pyramid Principle

The structuring approach we will look at is based on the *Pyramid Principle* by Barbara Minto, published in 1978 in a book of the same title. It is also known as the *Top-down Approach* and is one of the key tools used at McKinsey. The *Pyramid Principle* also states that "*ideas should always form a pyramid under a single thought.*" The single thought is the *hypothesis* — which could be the answer to a problem or a recommendation.

Underneath the *hypothesis*, you need to group and summarize the next level of supporting ideas, drivers, or questions. Then, for each supporting idea, driver, or question, break these down further, if necessary. Then put some structure and prioritization around them.

The general idea is that you break a problem into parts that can be analyzed more easily. Solutions or recommendations can then be developed for each part. In McKinsey-speak, this is called *disaggregating the problem.*

To build your *Pyramid*, you need to follow a 3-step approach:

1. Start with the answer or recommendation first (*Hypothesis*).
2. Group and summarize your supporting ideas/

drivers/arguments/questions.
3. Logically order your supporting ideas/drivers/
   arguments/questions.

A 'good' *Pyramid* (which is also known as *Issue Tree*) should contain three high-level drivers, issues, or questions. Potentially follows another layer of drivers, issues, or questions per high-level driver. By answering the questions related to the high-level drivers, you can very quickly determine the validity of your *hypothesis*. The issues or questions at each level should not overlap. Instead, they should be MECE (*Mutually Exclusive, Collectively Exhaustive* — we will get to the definition of this notion shortly).

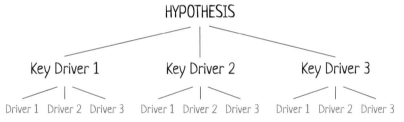

FIGURE 6

THE PYRAMID PRINCIPLE: ISSUE TREE WITH HYPOTHESIS & DRIVERS

Over time, I am sure you will learn to very much appreciate this *Pillar* of *Simplicity*. After all, the *Top-down Approach* is also very much in line with *common sense*.

Imagine you meet your boss, an executive, or a client in a hallway, and you are being asked, "*What should we do?*" The intuitively right thing to answer, "*We should do* X.", very crisply and directly. After that, you explain the reasons why. Ideally, you will give three reasons. And it just so happens that the magic number of drivers, ideas, or questions for each group of the *Pyramid* is three.

Along these lines, we will get to the *Rule of Three* shortly.

The below example of a *Pyramid* should make the approach more tangible for you. In this example related to cost savings, you see a set of *Key Drivers* under the *top-down hypothesis* associated with the reduction of *Operations Cost*. The *Key Drivers* are *Non-core Functions*, *Core Processes*, and *Supplier Cost*. For each, an initial hypothesis on potential cost savings has been developed. Under each *Key Driver*, you find an actionable approach on how to define the cost savings potential *bottom-up*. After you have identified the savings potential for each *Key Driver*, you can add these up, and you will then (hopefully) confirm the targeted savings of $5m. This is called *bottom-up verification* of the *top-down hypothesis*.

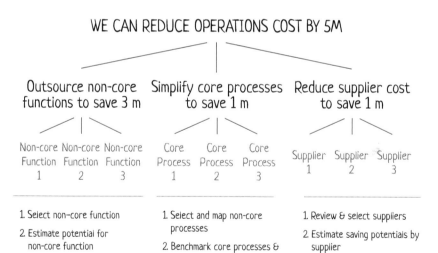

WE CAN REDUCE OPERATIONS COST BY 5M

Outsource non-core functions to save 3 m

Simplify core processes to save 1 m

Reduce supplier cost to save 1 m

| Non-core Function 1 | Non-core Function 2 | Non-core Function 3 | Core Process 1 | Core Process 2 | Core Process 3 | Supplier 1 | Supplier 2 | Supplier 3 |

Outsource non-core functions:
1. Select non-core function
2. Estimate potential for non-core function
3. Select outsourcing partners

Simplify core processes:
1. Select and map non-core processes
2. Benchmark core processes & identify best-practices
3. Adopt best-practices in core processes

Reduce supplier cost:
1. Review & select suppliers
2. Estimate saving potentials by supplier
3. Renegotiate with existing suppliers/chose alternative suppliers

FIGURE 7

THE PYRAMID PRINCIPLE: ISSUE TREE (EXAMPLE)

The application of the *Pyramid Principle* or *Issue Trees* is not only valuable to structure your thinking and prepare very focused problem-solving. It is also an excellent tool for structuring communications, for example, to your team, your managers, or your executives. We will explore this notion below, in our discussion of *Pillar #3*.

Speaking of tools — let's introduce two that are extremely helpful in developing a 'clean,' simple *Pyramid*, or *Issue Tree*: the *MECE Concept* and the *Rule of Three*.

The MECE Concept
(= Mutually Exclusive, Collectively Exhaustive)

Your *Pyramid* or *Issue Tree* helps you to wrap a structure around the available data and information by breaking the problem down into its parts (remember, this is called: *disaggregating the problem*). You structure a problem and break it down into pieces that are simple enough that you can handle (i.e., analyze) them relatively easily.

The best way to get your *Pyramid* or *Issue Tree* well-structured and 'clean' is to make sure that it is MECE. This means that all elements on every level of the *Pyramid* or *Tree* need to be *Mutually Exclusive* and *Collectively Exhaustive*. Or simply put: the different elements of the *Pyramid* or *Issue Tree* cannot overlap, yet they must cover all options of the spectrum of possibilities. This is another critical tool from the McKinsey tool kit.

A simple example of a MECE structure would be to categorize people by day of birth. Every person would land in one and only one category. An example of *non-MECE-ness* would be a categorization by nationality. Nationalities are neither *Mutually Exclusive* (some people have dual citizenship), nor *Collectively Exhaustive* (some people have none). These examples of MECE and *non*-MECE are illustrated below.

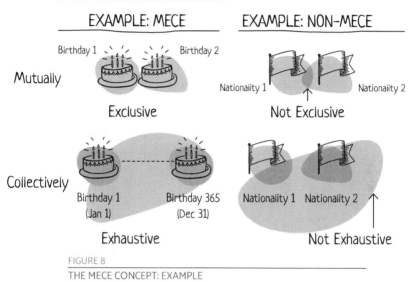

| EXAMPLE: MECE | EXAMPLE: NON-MECE |

FIGURE 8

THE MECE CONCEPT: EXAMPLE

There are three key benefits of making things MECE:

* Your structure is 'clean,' i.e., free of overlaps.
* Your structure is complete, i.e., you did not miss anything.
* It's possible to separately discuss or analyze every element of your structure because it is 'clean' and complete.

Make no mistake, however — making things MECE means making things simpler, so it is hard. Like with everything, though, with some practice, you should get the hang of it quite quickly.

Let's move on to the *Rule of Three*.

SIMPLICITY
TIP #8

WHEN STRUCTURING PROBLEMS, MAKE THINGS MECE (MUTUALLY EXCLUSIVE, COLLECTIVELY EXHAUSTIVE).

The Rule of Three

The *Rule of Three* is another potent yet simple tool. All you need to remember is that you try to *make all things come in Threes.* Apply this Rule when creating your *Issue Trees*, your presentations, or, more generally, in your communications. Whether you are preparing a speech, a marketing message, or when giving feedback in a performance review — try to make three points.

In fact, the *Rule of Three* is one of the oldest in the book — Aristotle wrote about it in his book Rhetoric. Put simply it is that people tend to easily remember three things, for example:

- The three reasons to support an argument
- The three steps to take next
- The three things someone does well (or not so well)

SIMPLICITY
TIP #9

TRY TO MAKE ALL THINGS COME IN THREES.

I am sure you can agree that the *Rule of Three* also makes intuitive (and, hence common) sense. Just think of the idiom that something is as *easy-as-1-2-3*. *Threes* are everywhere.

The key advantages of limiting yourself to *Three Things* are:

- People can quite easily remember them
- You force yourself to prioritize
- You strengthen your argument by being focused

While the *Rule of Three* itself is easy to remember, it's not quite so easy to apply. The tricky part lies in the second advantage mentioned above, i.e., that the *Rule* forces you to prioritize. That is easier said than done. You may have ten good reasons to support an argument, and now you need to distill those down to three.

Maybe you see the Top 3 reasons right away. For example, this could be the three sales channels with the highest revenue, so you focus on those (which is essentially an 80:20 *exercise* — more on the 80:20 *Rule* below, when we discuss *Pillar #2*).

But in many cases, it will not be that simple. Grouping your reasons may help, i.e., you can try to find three 'headlines' under which you can group your ten reasons.

At the same time, you should try to check whether your ten reasons are MECE. If not, you should be able to reduce your number of reasons. In other words, you need to decide whether the reasons are genuinely distinct or somehow 'overlapping' with each other. Make no mistake: this is hard, and there is no real recipe — you need to try, again and again, until you have broken things down to three.

While I have extensively highlighted the value of the *Rule of Three*: let's not be too 'dogmatic' about it. If you can only come up with two categories, or you need four, that's certainly not the end of the world. But at least <u>try</u> to get to three. And to conclude the topic, here one tip: it may help to introduce a fourth category named *Other*. This keeps you focused on the most important three, and you should still be able to keep things MECE.

SIMPLICITY
FACT #13

THE RULE OF THREE IS SO VALUABLE BECAUSE PEOPLE CAN EASILY REMEMBER THREE THINGS AND BECAUSE IT FORCES PRIORITIZATION.

Practice, Practice, Practice

As indicated, the application of Pillar #1 – Problem Structuring – requires quite some practice until you get the hang of it. In fact, this is probably the one approach in this book that is most difficult to understand and apply. Especially tackling Steps 1 and 2 – defining the key hypothesis and identifying/structuring the supporting ideas/drivers/questions – can be quite a challenge in the beginning. Don't give up! Remind yourself again of Steve Jobs' words:

*"You have to work hard to get your thinking
clean to make it simple.
But it's worth it in the end because once you get
there, you can move mountains."*

So please bear with me through the next few pages — it is worth it!

Forming an initial hypothesis will make problem-solving more efficient and more effective. But to reap these benefits, you need to be able to first generate these hypotheses and then test them.

The definition of the hypothesis happens at the start of the problem-solving process. At that point, you are likely not to have much data (since you will not have done much data gathering, yet).

Remember, you don't want to do a lot of digging before you've defined what you should dig for. Instead, you need to first review all readily available, high-level data and information on the problem at hand — individually or as a team. These 'quick and dirty' insights you need to combine with your *common sense* and develop a hypothesis or hypotheses on the most likely outcome(s) or solution(s).

Your initial hypothesis may turn out to be wrong, but that's ok — it's the starting point you need. Once you have generated the hypothesis, you can define which analyses you have to perform and which questions you need to ask to prove or disprove your hypothesis.

This will provide you with a road map, albeit a hastily sketched one, that takes you from problem to solution. If your initial hypothesis is correct, then solving the problem means filling in the details of the map through factual analysis. If your initial hypothesis turns out to be wrong, no worries: your analyses will lead you to the right solution.

To illustrate this approach from an entirely different angle: what medical doctors call *differential diagnosis* is also nothing but a *hypothesis-based approach*. A patient coming to a practice or hospital will report on specific symptoms. The doctor will then develop a hypothesis of the possible diagnosis. Based on this hypothesis, the doctor will the ask specific questions and conduct targeted exams. Mainly following the *Pyramid Principle*, the doctor will then either prove the hypothesis or will reach the point where only one candidate disease or condition remains probable.

To more clearly illustrate what challenge you are likely to face in getting the hang of this approach, let me share a story from my own past. Very early on in my career as a McKinsey consultant, we had a 3-week training called the Mini-MBA (for all the rookies without a formal MBA). On several occasions during this training, we went through the following exercise:

1. Receive tons of information on company X
   (a 1-2 feet pile of paper).
2. Develop a recommendation whether company X
   should do this or that.
3. You have 2-3 hours ...

As you can imagine, at first, yours truly and fellow consultant rookies were somewhere between disbelief and panic. There was barely enough time to properly skim through all the documents, much less read them. So how should we reach any reasonable recommendation? This entire exercise seemed crazy.

Fast forward a few years, I have developed a sort

of 'x-ray vision' when it comes to business problems. But it took me many engagements as a consultant and projects in senior line roles to develop this 'x-ray vision.'

Today, I can quickly figure out what to look for when faced with the equivalent of '1-2 feet of paper.' Usually, it will then take me no more than a few hours (sometimes even just minutes) to come up with a hypothesis on whether to do this or that (and why).

Similarly, in any new client or work situation, I am typically able to detect specific business strengths or challenges within only weeks or even days. These are most frequently related to tools, processes, or organizational aspects.

The bottom-line: all it takes to master the *hypothesis-based approach* is *common sense* and some practice—then you can start to "*move mountains*" .

Bringing Pillar #1 to Life
A Practical Example on Problem Structuring

The above may sound a little theoretical and is certainly not easy to 'digest, ' especially when you read it for the first time. Let me add some 'color' to this approach by sharing a relatively simple real-life example with you.

This example goes back to the very beginning of my career in business. In fact, it goes back to my very first day as a management consultant. We were working for a major global player in the high-tech industry. The goal of our engagement was to help the client save money in the procurement of their *Indirect Materials*. These are everything you need to run the business outside of the actual manufacturing or production process, such as laptops, software, or all kinds of services.

Based on what we have discussed above, we needed to start the creation of our pyramid or issue tree by defining a key hypothesis. In our case, we brought in a senior partner with a lot of procurement experience who assessed the situation based on initial discussions and his expertise. He formulated the key hypothesis:

We can save 10% on indirect materials.

Ok – so now we had a hypothesis. The next question was how to structure the problem to prove or disprove this hypothesis. Since we were looking at *Indirect Materials*, we started by discussing how we could structure those into several categories. We identified 3+1 high-level categories that were MECE:

1. Hardware
2. Software
3. Services
4. Other

As you can see, we just 'broke' the *Rule of Three* by introducing *Other* as a fourth category. Like in most cases, the category *Other* turned out to be of minor relevance, so we will eliminate it for the remainder of this example.

To be able to make things more specific, we broke each of the three high-level categories down into 2-3 further ones that were again MECE. As a result, we created the following pyramid.

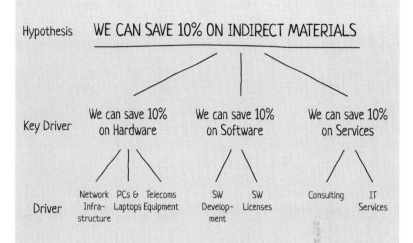

Hypothesis — WE CAN SAVE 10% ON INDIRECT MATERIALS

Key Driver — We can save 10% on Hardware | We can save 10% on Software | We can save 10% on Services

Driver — Network Infrastructure | PCs & Laptops | Telecoms Equipment | SW Development | SW Licenses | Consulting | IT Services

FIGURE 9
CASE EXAMPLE: ISSUE TREE FOR PROCUREMENT SPEND

To simplify things, we would assume at this stage that we could save 10% on every category. With that, the problem was adequately structured and ready for analysis.

A personal note: In case you continue to struggle as you practice this hypothesis-driven approach, you may want to find yourself a coach. Maybe you can find a former management consultant who is well versed in-house. Else, please also feel free to reach out to me (my email address is indicated in the section on the *Simplicity for Success* book series). I am sure we can find a way to help you.

CHAPTER 8

PILLAR #2: ANALYSIS

"DECIDING WHAT NOT TO DO IS AS IMPORTANT
AS DECIDING WHAT TO DO."

STEVE JOBS

You have just defined the key questions you need to answer to prove (or disprove) your hypothesis. Now, you can go ahead and identify the required analyses. However, before you start with your analyses, you need to prioritize which ones are most important. You only need to conduct the analyses that prove or disprove your hypothesis — no more, no less.

In other words: it is critical that you get your analytical priorities straight. Otherwise you risk 'boiling the ocean', i.e., to spend many hours conducting analyses and creating results that do not create relevant insights. Not a good idea — time and resources are always limited.

Prioritizing your analyses will also help you to focus only on data that is most relevant for these. Obtaining and preparing data for analyses can be a very time-consuming challenge, as we have discussed in Chapter 5.

So which analyses are 'high priority' and which ones are 'nice-to-have'? To prioritize, you need to do three things simultaneously:

1. Keep looking at the *Big Picture*
2. Identify (and prioritize) the *Key Drivers*
3. Apply the 80:20 *Rule* (I will explain this rule shortly)

Start by identifying which analyses are *quick wins*, i.e., easy to conduct and likely to make a significant contribution to proving (or disproving) your *hypothesis*.

SIMPLICITY

TIP #10

TO PRIORITIZE YOUR ANALYSES, DO THREE THINGS SIMULTANEOUSLY:
1. KEEP LOOKING AT THE BIG PICTURE
2. IDENTIFY (AND PRIORITIZE) THE KEY DRIVERS
3. APPLY THE 80:20 RULE

To avoid losing sight of the *Big Picture*, keep revisiting your *Initial Hypothesis* and *Issue Tree*. Take the metaphorical step back and remind yourself what it is that you are trying to achieve. Ask yourself (again and again) how specific analyses fit into the *Big Picture* and how they can help you solve your problem. This will help you to identify and focus on the most critical analyses.

Which brings me to the *Key Drivers*. Every business, business model, or process is affected by many factors, but only driven by a limited number of most critical ones, namely the *Key Drivers*.

As you prioritize your analyses, it is essential to identify the *Key Drivers*. Focusing on these means drilling down directly to the core of the problem, rather than picking the whole problem apart piece by piece, layer by layer. Ignoring the less relevant factors is your only hope to not get lost in detail.

Conducting your analyses: Keep it simple!

Once you have obtained the data for your prioritized analyses, you can put it in a spreadsheet, Pivot table, or Access database. This allows you to analyze and 'slice & dice' it in various ways. You will then typically begin to see patterns that highlight aspects of the business that may not have been obvious at the start.

Please note that I deliberately said 'spreadsheet, Pivot table, or Access database'. In my experience, even today, you can address and analyze most key business challenges without sophisticated software tools, *Data Science*, or even AI. The more advanced tools may come in handy (or may be necessary under certain circumstances). But generally, you should assume that you can pull data from whatever relevant source and analyze it using relatively standard tools.

Another critical consideration I would like to highlight is that creating transparency through analyses is one of the most essential keys to *Simplicity*. I have been in many meetings where managers tried to make decisions without having the most important analyses at hand. As a result, everybody was trying to push decisions based on 'arbitrary' numbers or directly 'from the gut.' Typically, you will spend about 80% of your time working on creating transparency, i.e., problem structuring and analyses. This is where the 'heavy-lifting' takes place. Yet once you have done this successfully, the *SoWhats*, recommendations, or necessary next steps can be identified quite easily.

Again: simple is hard!

SIMPLICITY
FACT #14

CREATING TRANSPARENCY IS ONE OF THE MOST ESSENTIAL KEYS TO SIMPLICITY – AND TYPICALLY REQUIRES 80% OF THE OVERALL EFFORT.

Simplify your results:
Don't try to be precise

In addition to the above, you can often simplify the results of your analyses, especially in presentations, by not trying to be precise. This notion may surprise you in the context of data-based analyses that are supposed to be the foundation for sound business decision-making.

For engineers and scientists, this thought may even be painful: how could you not want the results of your analyses to be precise? Let's face it: business, unlike physics or math, is, for the most part, not an exact science. In school and in college, we have been trained to be precise – and that's mostly a good thing.

Science and engineering require precision. When you're calculating a trajectory to Mars, you want to make sure that you go into orbit around it instead of crashing into it. Don't laugh: this really happened to NASA's Mars Climate Orbiter in 1999, due to an error in converting numbers between the SI (or Metric) System and United States Customary Units.

Also, in budgeting or accounting, you want to be

reasonably sure that you're not off by too many percent, especially if you are talking about millions or billions of dollars.

But most strategic and operational business decisions require far less precision. In fact, trying to make business decisions based on a scientific level of exactitude is mostly inefficient. Usually, you can obtain an answer that is directionally correct and of the right order of magnitude very quickly. Attaining spurious 'precision' takes much longer, with little to no value add.

Trying to be precise is like 'boiling the ocean': an excessive amount of time and effort is consumed by your analyses. This is especially true with forward-looking analyses, such as forecasts. Any number that you come up with will most likely be wrong anyway, since you are modeling based on a set of assumptions.

As Nobel laureate in Physics, Niels Bohr, once famously said:

> *"Prediction is very difficult,*
> *especially if it's about the future."*

While I was still in grad school, we used to call this 'pseudo-accuracy'. Forget about showing a number like 9,984.56 on a slide. Rather round numbers up or down and show them in the simplest possible way. Write: 10,000. Or even better — indicate 'in '000' in the title and then simply write 10. That's within 1% of the precise number — just so much easier to read and 'digest.'

I can't count the number of analyses or presentations I have seen for which it was close to impossible to efficiently derive a SoWhat. In most cases, the sole reason was that there were too many numbers and digits on them.

SIMPLICITY

TIP #11

DON'T TRY TO BE PRECISE IN BUSINESS ANALYSES –MAKE THINGS EASIER TO GRASP BY ROUNDING NUMBERS.

In any case — and in most cases — it is best to graphically depict the results of your analyses, for example, by using bar charts or waterfall charts. It's so much easier to get a feel for quantities from graphical analyses, rather than tables of numbers. And very often, you will be able to easily derive a *SoWhat* from a graphical analysis. Being able to see proportions or ratios makes interpretation and prioritization so much easier.

SIMPLICITY

TIP #12

TO BE ABLE TO MORE EFFICIENTLY DERIVE SOWHATS, CREATE GRAPHS (E.G., AS BAR CHARTS) RATHER THAN TABLES.

Which is a great moment to talk about the 80:20 *Rule*.

Prioritization: The 80:20 Rule

The power of *Simplicity* also lies in the ability to figure out what is essential and what is not. This is where the 80:20 *Rule* — one of the great truths of all things business — comes in handy. You could call it a cousin of the normal distribution from statistics. It is based on the observation that the lion's share of the effect comes from a relatively small number of causes.

The 80:20 *Rule* was originally developed by Italian economist Vilfredo Pareto in the 19th Century (hence also called the Pareto Principle). It was more recently popularized by Richard Koch, who wrote the book The 80/20 Principle in the mid-1990s. To play with some words: this principle is as real as the law of gravity, yet most people fail to see its gravity.

SIMPLICITY
FACT #15

THE 80:20 RULE
IS BASED ON THE
OBSERVATION THAT
THE LION'S SHARE OF THE
EFFECT COMES FROM A
RELATIVELY SMALL
NUMBER OF CAUSES.

You can apply the 80:20 Rule across all functions of your business (from Procurement via Product Development all the way to Marketing & Sales) and even in your personal life. Here, we will focus on how you can leverage the 80:20 *Rule* for analyses.

As you conduct your analyses, you will find the 80:20 *Rule* proven many times over, for example, when you find things such as

- 80% of sales come from 20% of sales people
- 80% of orders come from 20% of customers

The 80:20 *Rule* is all about data. And data is the key to answering the questions that you have created along your *Issue Tree*, such as

- What are the sales figures by product type?
- What is the margin by product type?
- What does the geographical distribution of customers look like?

Let me give you a real-life example of the power of the 80:20 *Rule*. During one of my adventures, I became part of the new strategy department of a multi-billion $ family business. A major consultancy had been working on a growth strategy for about a year. They had identified 46 initiatives that should be pursued to grow the business by 20% over the coming 5 years. Anyone with even a little bit of experience in managing a portfolio of initiatives will just have been shaking their head when reading the number 46.

Under hardly any circumstances, regardless of the size of the business, would it make sense to drive and track such a vast number of growth initiatives. I went back to the responsible partner of that consultancy. I asked him for an analysis of the Top 10 growth initiatives and their expected revenue impact. After not receiving the analysis after a few days, I requested the spreadsheet with all the data (which was duly sent).

I spent about half an hour with the spreadsheet. I then found that — drum roll — the Top 10 initiatives were expected to contribute about 80% of the revenue growth. Of course: 80:20. Action taken: focus on the Top 10 initiatives and forget about the other 36 (at least for the time being).

A great side effect of the 80:20 *Rule* and mindset is

that you will almost automatically be able to identify the famous 'low-hanging fruits.' Often, you'll still be in the middle of the problem-solving process when you find opportunities for an easy win, for example, through immediate improvements. Seize those opportunities.

Harvesting that 'low-hanging fruit' typically gives you added credibility, makes your management (or client) happy, plus it's an indication that you are on the right track. Imagine you are working on a project or initiative that is meant to last three months and you come up with immediately implementable actions after only two weeks — this will not only make you look really good, but also will help you to more easily obtain buy-in for future recommendations. Don't wait — harvest the 'low hanging fruit,' then continue working on the more comprehensive solution.

SIMPLICITY

TIP #13

ALWAYS TRY TO USE THE 80:20 RULE TO PRIORITIZE AND IDENTIFY LOW-HANGING FRUIT.

Conducting the Analyses and identifying the SoWhats

Once you have prioritized your analyses, it is time to get going. Before you can conduct the actual analyses, you need to answer 3 questions:

1. Does the necessary data exist?
2. How can you access the data?
3. Does the data have to be 'prepared'?

These questions seem trivial, but in practice, they are very often far from that. Ideally, you find the owner of the data, who 'pulls' it for you, and you plug it into a spreadsheet and conduct your analyses.

More often than not, it is not quite that easy. You may find that the necessary data is not readily available. Depending on the type of data, you may find yourself running, for example, from Finance to Marketing to IT in search of the data. Worst case, the data does not exist, which means that you cannot conduct a specific analysis.

SIMPLICITY
FACT #16

TO BE ABLE TO EFFECTIVELY CONDUCT AN ANALYSIS, THE NECESSARY DATA:
1. NEEDS TO EXIST
2. NEEDS TO BE EASILY ACCESSIBLE
3. SHOULD NOT REQUIRE MUCH PREPARATION (E.G., CLEANSING

In practice, data is often not of the expected quality (e.g., with the data from specific periods or regions missing) and/ or may need significant preparation (i.e., data cleansing). This may be both time-consuming and costly and may also become a showstopper for your analysis.

Let's assume that you're able to conduct your analyses. You should still be mindful of the fact that, depending on the quality and completeness of the input data, the reliability of your results may be limited.

While you typically don't need to be precise (as discussed), you certainly want to be sufficiently accurate (i.e., at least in the right ballpark). Hence you need to sanity check every analysis before you start identifying the SoWhats.

Most probably, you will not have the time to perform a detailed check on every analysis your team or your colleagues produce. This is where sanity checks come in. These are crucial because we sometimes have the tendency to blindly believe the results of an analysis — that's dangerous (remember: *Garbage In — Garbage Out*). You always need to quickly ensure that the result of an analysis is plausible.

Although there is no one best way to do a sanity check, you typically will want to check whether your quantitative results make some sense in the big scheme of things. Hence, *common sense* is your best friend again.

Ask yourself things like: Is the overall revenue in the right ballpark? Does the calculated target price make sense? Is the growth rate realistic? If sales numbers seem to have increased or decreased by hundreds of percent or if your computation shows that you should quadruple the price of a product, probably something is wrong. So you better double-check both your data and your model.

In any case, it is always best to have an outsider do the sanity check or ask a few probing questions. This should be someone who has not been directly involved in conducting the analysis. In most cases, this outsider will help you quickly identify if any results seem odd.

SIMPLICITY
TIP #14

SANITY CHECK EVERY ANALYSIS FOR PLAUSIBILITY BEFORE YOU START TO TRY TO IDENTIFY SOWHATS.

Once the results of an analysis have been sanity-checked, it's time to identify the *SoWhats*. As you run through the results of your analyses, you will most certainly find that some of them are dead ends: interesting outcomes, but no real insights.

This is likely to happen in many cases, even if the analyses had been prioritized. You need to figure out which of your analyses provide the most impactful insights (these we call the 'killer analyses') and which ones turn out to be irrelevant. To achieve this, you need to look at the results of every single analysis and ask yourself, *SoWhat?*

In other words: you need to figure out what specific results are telling you and whether these insights are useful. For example, you need to identify whether a particular result leads to a specific recommendation.

Bottom line: you can discard analyses which have no *SoWhat*. And you need to synthesize all *SoWhats* from your analyses into insights and, ultimately, recommendations and an action plan.

Bringing Pillar #2 to Life
A Practical Example on Analysis

At the end of this chapter, let me try again to make things more tangible by sharing the next steps we took in the simple real-life example, we started to discuss in Chapter 7. We had formulated the key hypothesis:

We can save 10% on indirect materials.

Also, we had structured the problem and had defined three high-level categories (*Software*, *Hardware*, *Services*), along with a total of eight categories.

The question now would be: how much can we really save in procurement cost for each of the categories? To find an answer to this question, we would first have to figure out the current spend by subcategory. To keep things easy to analyze, we decided to look at total spending for the past year.

While you would assume that obtaining and analyzing this kind of data should be straightforward, it turned out to be the biggest hurdle we encountered during this engagement. The data was distributed across different business units, and every business unit used a different generation of the same software tool. We were initially told that it was impossible to pull the data in a standardized structure and format.

To make a long story short, we found a way to pull the data from the different systems in the same structure and format. This data was entered into an Access database, and an 'Access guru' prepared the database within a few days, enabling us to efficiently conduct the necessary analyses.

Since we did not know in advance what we would find, we had defined a whole list of procurement parameters that might be worth looking at. This list included everything from the type of item or service bought, the product category, the name of the supplier, the purchasing business unit, the date of purchase, all the way to, of course, the amount paid.

With the Access database at hand, we could now easily create the spending analysis shown below along the different categories. From the bar charts, you can quickly derive that, in the first step, we were focusing on three spending categories: *Network Infrastructure, SW Development, and IT Services*. These three made up about 80% of all spending.

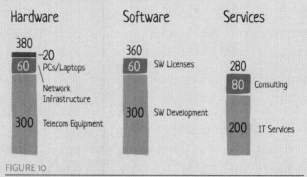

FIGURE 10
CASE EXAMPLE: SPEND ANALYSIS BY CATEGORY

Now that we knew where to focus, the next step was to zoom in on these three categories. We needed to get a better understanding of how much could possibly be saved by category and how these savings could be realized. One of the avenues we pursued was to look at the spending breakdown by supplier for each category. As a result, we created the following analyses. As you can easily see, each category was dominated by 1-2 major suppliers, plus a lot of *Others*.

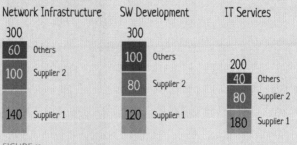

FIGURE 11
CASE EXAMPLE: SPEND ANALYSIS BY SUBCATEGORY

Based on these analyses, deriving the *SoWhats* was relatively straightforward:

1. You could go back to major *Suppliers 1 & 2* for *Network Infrastructure*, *SW Development*, and *IT Services* to renegotiate the price.
2. You could try to largely eliminate the category *Others* under *Network Infrastructure* by buying the required products at a lower price from *Suppliers 1 & 2*.
3. Similarly, you could explore the possibility of purchasing *SW Development and IT Services* under *Others* at a lower price from *Suppliers 1 & 2*.

Of course, in a second step, we would also explore easy ways to save on spending for smaller categories such as *PCs/Laptops*, *SW Licenses*, or *Consulting*. But for *Simplicity's* sake, we will not look at these categories here.

With that, we had completed the prioritization and our most critical analyses and were ready for story-lining and decision-making.

CHAPTER 9

PILLAR #3: STORY-LINING & DECISION-MAKING

> "IF YOU CAN'T EXPLAIN IT TO A SIX-YEAR-OLD,
> YOU DON'T UNDERSTAND IT YOURSELF."
>
> —ALBERT EINSTEIN

The Concept of Top-down Storytelling

Now that you have completed your analyses, it is time to share your wisdom with the world. Let's discuss how to best tell the story of your key findings (*SoWhats*) to ensure that your audience can follow your logic and buys into your recommendations.

The simple, yet magic, key to story-lining is that you follow the *Top-down Approach*. Telling a story *top-down* is as critical as it is powerful since it helps you focus your audience on what is most important. Most of us are not aware of it, but through most of our lives, we are trained to tell stories *bottom-up*. This is due to the scientific approach we are typically taught in college and grad school. First, we state the problem, then we define the experiment, we conduct the experiment, we analyze the results, and then, finally, we derive the conclusions.

Yet, in life and in business, the only thing that is of real relevance, especially to business leaders, is the key findings and recommendations. Managers and executives always focus on decision-making. They want to understand from their teams which decisions they should make and why. They want to see options and rationales.

So, logically, you should start your story or presentation with your key findings and recommendations. But most of us have simply not been trained that way. We tend to overload our managers and executives with tons of data, diligently sharing all possible insights and results of our analyses *bottom-up*. Then we expect our managers and executives to absorb and understand all the details we have compiled for them over days or weeks within a ½-hour or an hour. And, finally, we expect them to derive the *SoWhats* and make the necessary decisions on the spot, after they had literally only minutes to absorb and digest all our insights.

That's the wrong approach. And it's almost guaranteed to make your managers and executives extremely frustrated.

SIMPLICITY
TIP #15

CREATE STORYLINES AND PRESENTATIONS THAT FOLLOW THE TOP-DOWN APPROACH.

Let me share another little story along these lines. While I was heading the strategy department at a major conglomerate, a finance colleague approached me regarding an upcoming presentation. One of the world's leading real estate consultancies was to present to our CEO and the leadership team.

This colleague asked me to review the draft slide deck that the consultants had provided for a planned one-hour presentation and give her feedback. So I did. For starters, the deck was way too long, 60 pages. And then the story was told bottom-up, i.e., all the key findings and recommendations were after page 50.

My recommendations were (1) to shorten the deck to 20-30 pages and (2) to tell the story *top-down*, i.e., to start with the key findings.

When the presentation took place, I was surprised to find the deck unchanged. The board room was filled, the CEO sitting at the top end of the table — let the show begin.

And what happened next was what I expected: after about 15 pages and 30 minutes, the CEO asked for the key findings — which were to be presented 'shortly.' With 10 minutes and 25 pages to go, the CEO said he would have to leave soon. Then the 60 minutes were over, but the key findings and recommendations hadn't been presented.

Looking at the 20 people in the room, a quite disgruntled CEO asked to reschedule for another time and left the room. He had neither heard the key findings, nor was he enabled to decide what's next. Had the story been told *top-down*, this situation would have been avoided.

All managers and executives are busy people. They are perpetually short on time, are used to processing lots of information quickly, and get impatient when they feel like someone isn't getting to the point. That's why you want to make your recommendations first and foremost.

Many executives think in a *top-down* manner, so they want to focus on the *Big Picture* and concrete recommendations. They don't want to get bogged down by details first. By delivering your recommendation in the 'answer first' format, you are fitting into the executive's mental model and allowing them to quickly process it.

To sum it up: the primary purpose of story-lining is to enable decision-making. Hence you need to:

- Tell the story top-down
- Provide options for decision-making, and recommend one specific choice
- Base this recommendation on the key findings (e.g., listing the pros and cons per option)

To do this, you can structure your storyline along the *Pyramid* or *Issue Tree* you created during problem structuring (see *Pillar #1*).

Decision-making:
Clear Options & Recommendations

Decision-making sounds so important. Isn't everyone dreaming of being a powerful CEO, sitting in a fancy boardroom and making important decisions?

The reality is much less glorious. I remember sitting with the CFO of a multi-billion\$ business in his — not-at-all glorious — office one evening. The building was empty, and it was already dark outside. The CFO suddenly started to reflect, talking to himself: "*I wonder how many of the decisions we are making in the board are actually getting implemented? I am wildly guessing that it's around 50% ...*"

The reflections of this CFO point at the three fundamental challenges associated with decision making:

- You need to make the right decisions
- You need to make sure that your team understands your decisions (and the required actions)
- You need to ensure that your decisions get implemented

This again sounds simple, yet it is tough to achieve. Still, *Simplicity* is your best ally in meeting these three challenges:

- You are likely to make the right decisions if you have conducted the right analyses and if the results of these analyses are embedded in a simple, concise storyline (along with actionable options and recommendations).
- Your team is likely to understand the decision also based on the simple, concise storyline, including the analyses, options, and recommendations — complemented by concrete, simple instructions on actions and next steps.
- You are likely to ensure implementation if you ask your team for a simple implementation plan, including required activities, timelines, and owners, and then regularly follow-up on status.

Sounds simple enough, but you will not believe how many times I've seen organizations struggle with the above. I recently talked to the former CTO of a major high-tech company about this. He told me: "*These were exactly the situations when I brought in consultants. When an organization struggles in terms of capacity or capability – that's when you need to bring in external help (with a clearly defined mandate).*"

SIMPLICITY
TIP #16

IF YOU NEED AN EXECUTIVE DECISION, PROVIDE OPTIONS, ALONG WITH PROS AND CONS FOR EACH, AND RECOMMENDWHICH OPTION TO PURSUE.

Along these lines, let me share another – more uplifting – story. During the first week on a new job, one of my new team members approached me regarding a presentation to be given to the chairman of the organization the following week. She put a 200-page consultant report in front of me and asked: "*Could you please give me some guidance on which of these slides we should present to the chairman next week?*"

I had absolutely no idea what this was all about, so I asked her to give me some context and describe the objective of the meeting with the chairman. I absorbed her explanations, then I gave her my answer: "*We are not going to use any of these 200 slides.*" She looked flabbergasted. Then I wanted to know how much time we would have with the chairman. Her answer:

"30 *minutes*." Accordingly, I advised her to create the following four slides:

- Slide 1: *Situation* — Remind the chairman of the context and why we are with him.
- Slide 2-3: *Key Results*— Explain the key findings from the consultant report to the chairman.
- Slide 4: *Recommendation & Next Steps* — Outline three possible options on the next steps, address pros & cons, recommend one option, and obtain a decision.

Simple, right?! The next day I walked by my team member's desk to check in on her: "*How is it going?*" She gave me a long hard look and rolled her eyes: "*This is hard!*" I burst out laughing: "*I know.*" Then we sketched out the four pages together. After two more iterations, our mini-presentation was ready.

The meeting with the chairman went smooth as silk. We presented the three options regarding next steps, clearly indicating the pros and cons of each option. He approved the option we had recommended. After only 11 minutes, we left the room. The power of *Simplicity* in action — but: getting to these four simple slides was hard work indeed.

To sum it up: at the executive management level, there is a clear expectation that presentations be clear and concise. Stories need to be told *top-down*, and the resulting recommendations need to have a clear rationale, based on targeted, often simple, analyses. This is driven by the fact that executive managers have so many issues to deal with. Hence, their only chance to make educated decisions on all these issues is that every aspect — and especially the recommendations — are presented clearly and concisely.

Yet, so many times, I have seen executive leaders who were highly frustrated by being overwhelmed with data and information, while not being provided with clear recommendations. This is often the result of challenges at the senior-/mid-management level. I have seen many VPs and directors who were very aware that their executives wanted simple presentations that tell the story top-down. At the same time, these same VPs and directors were overwhelmed with data and analyses by their teams. As a result, they would have to be the ones to distill and simplify all this information and create an executive-level storyline. However, since simple is hard, in most cases, they do not have the time to make things simple.

The challenge is then to get out of a *catch*-22 situation and create a *virtuous cycle*. Whether you are a VP, director, manager or analyst, applying the tools of *Simplicity* can make you successful.

As a manager or analyst, you want to structure and prioritize your analyses, ask yourself for the *SoWhats, and try* to identify *killer analyses* or *low-hanging fruits*. If you pursue this approach and share these results with your manager, you are guaranteed to 'harvest' delight.

Similarly, as a director or manager, you want to create a *top-down* storyline and identify and prioritize the necessary analyses yourself. This will tremendously help your managers and analysts in focusing their efforts on the most relevant analyses.

If you make this a team effort, after a few iterations, you are likely to create a *virtuous cycle* that will benefit all. At all levels, you are likely to waste less time, be more focused, and, ultimately, help yourself to advance your career. I have also seen this happen many times over.

'Every-day' Decisions: Simple Rules

Decision-making doesn't just happen at the top of an organization. Every day, employees at all levels need to make a vast number of decisions. To ensure consistency in decision-making, you need to define rules, both with regards to internal processes and, even more importantly, with regards to customer interactions. To facilitate smooth and consistent decision-making, it is a good idea to define *Simple Rules* for all relevant team members.

An example of not having simple decision-making rules was something I experienced during another professional 'adventure.' At the time, I was asked to join a meeting where a new onboarding and training process for newly recruited sales reps was to be presented. The training constituted a substantial investment by the company, and based on experience, some of the new hires did not take this training too seriously. Hence, the focus of the discussion was on rules to identify the not-too-serious recruits (and, subsequently, ask them to leave).

The proposed solution was a complicated point system, along the lines of: *if-you-do-this-or-that-you-get-X-points-and-if-you-reach-Y-points-you-have-to-leave-the-programs-but-you-can-make-up-points-by-doing-this-or-that*. The entire approach was confusing and spanned several pages of a presentation.

During the discussion, I highlighted that not only was the approach too complicated, but also, many rules were ambiguous. Hence, it was guaranteed that there would be lots of controversy around the application of the rules.

My recommendation was: "*If you want this concept to*

be successful, create a set of rules that fits on one page and can be grasped by the average new sales rep in less than a minute — tough, but fair."

I even remember making a concrete suggestion along these lines. This suggestion was dismissed by the leaders in charge. The result was continued issues, and the careers of these 'leaders' at this company were short-lived.

SIMPLICITY
TIP #17

FOR EVERY-DAY DECISIONS, PROVIDE SIMPLE RULES.

To sum it up: to obtain decisions from executives, you need to follow the *Three Pillars of Simplicity*. Start by structuring the problem at hand, then conduct the most relevant (= prioritized) analyses, and develop a *top-down storyline*. The storyline needs to include concrete recommendations (potentially with different options to choose from) for decision by your leadership.

When it comes to the *every-day decisions*, you need to introduce simple rules to ensure consistency in decision-making across the company. These rules not only need to be inherently simple, but they also need to be limited in number. Capping the number of rules and keeping the rules simple makes them easy to remember and maintains a focus on what matters most.

Bringing Pillar #3 to Life
A Practical Example on Story-lining & Decision-making

At the end of this chapter, let me again try to add some 'color' to this approach by continuing to share the next steps we took in our real-life example. We had come up with the three *SoWhats*:

1. Go back to major *Suppliers 1 and 2* for *Network Infrastructure*, *SW Development*, and *IT Services* to renegotiate the price.
2. Try to largely eliminate the category *Others* under *Network Infrastructure* by buying the particular products at a better price from *Suppliers 1 and 2*.
3. Explore the possibility of purchasing *SW Development & IT Services* under *Others* at a better price from *Suppliers 1 and 2*.

Based on these *SoWhats*, we now needed to develop a *top-down storyline* and recommend decisions and next steps to be taken.

In our real-life example, we had to go back to the procurement leadership team to test for each category, whether the 10% savings from our hypothesis were achievable. Even more importantly, we had to address the how.

Specifically, that means that we had to dig deeper and discuss every *SoWhat* in the context of the 10% savings-hypothesis. For example, we would have to address questions such as:

- What does the current contract with *Supplier 1* for *Network Infrastructure* look like?
- Would we expect *Supplier 1* to be willing to renegotiate?
- In a renegotiation, which price reduction should we target: 5%, 10%, 15%?

- What negotiation levers could we bring to the table? (One approach we discussed was: *"If you are willing to give us a better price, we may buy more from you next year."* Another one was: *"The contract is expiring next year, so if you are not willing to discuss price now, we may buy from the competition.")*?
- Which products that we are currently buying from *Others* could we buy at a better price from *Supplier* 1 instead?

The final story we came up with is summarized in the below waterfall slide (in which the numbers are, of course, just illustrative). The — *top-down* — story was:

1. We believe that savings of 10%, i.e., of $102K, are possible for the procurement of *indirect materials*.
2. To realize these savings, we request your approval (1) to renegotiate with some suppliers and (2) to shift some procurement to larger suppliers. (*Wave* 1)
3. Since these measures are expected to result in total savings of only about 8% (i.e., $76K), we would target to realize an additional savings amount of $26K from a *Wave* 2.

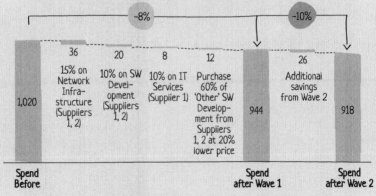

FIGURE 12

CASE EXAMPLE: WATERFALL OF POTENTIAL SAVINGS

As you can see, the final storyline is quite straightforward and simple, yet getting to this point took quite a lot of hard work.

I hope that this practical example helped illustrate to use the *Three Pillars of Simplicity*.

And again: as you practice the application of the *Three Pillars of Simplicity*, find yourself a coach, for example, a colleague who is a former management consultant and may be able to help. And always feel free to reach out to me (you can find my email address in the section on the *Simplicity for Success* book series).

CONCLUSION
SIMPLICITY
FOR YOUR SUCCESS

"THE SECRET OF GETTING AHEAD IS GETTING
STARTED. THE SECRET OF GETTING STARTED IS
BREAKING YOUR COMPLEX, OVERWHELMING TASKS
INTO SMALL MANAGEABLE TASKS
AND THEN STARTING ON THE FIRST ONE."

— MARK TWAIN

S *implicity* is probably the most neglected managerial art, on the one hand, because of people's fear of being considered simple-minded, on the other hand, because it's so hard to achieve.

To get an analysis, a presentation, or a product or service offering truly simple, you need to overcome your own complicating habits. And you may have to fight the business culture around you.

In the chapters of this book, I have provided you with an introductory overview of the power of *Simplicity*. We have discussed why *Simplicity* is hard to achieve but impactful. We have explored why *Simplicity* is even more critical in the age of *Big Data*, *Data Science*, and AI. We have also looked at the *Magic Tool of Simplicity*, *The Three Pillars*. We have looked at these *Pillars* in quite some detail to explain how to structure, prioritize, and conduct analyses, and then develop *top-down storylines* that enable 'educated decision-making'. In the process, I introduced you to a variety of powerful *Simplicity* tools, such as:

- The *Virtuous Cycle of Simplicity*:
  Structure – Prioritize – Iterate
- The *Magic Tool of Simplicity*: Problem Solving
- The *Pyramid Principle*
- The 'MECE' Concept
  (= '*Mutually Exclusive, Collectively Exhaustive*')
- The *Rule of Three*
- The 80:20 *Rule*
- The *Top-down Approach*, esp. for storytelling

I hope that I could convince you of the power of *Simplicity*. I know that, quipped with the above tools, you are already in the position to successfully leverage *Simplicity* by tackling business challenges such as:

- Structuring and prioritizing a problem using an issue tree and based on an initial hypothesis.
- Analyzing data effectively and efficiently (based on prioritized analyses) and drawing the right conclusions (or *SoWhats*).
- Creating and communicating story lines *top-down*.

If you are courageous and persistent enough, I can almost guarantee you that leveraging *Simplicity* will make you successful, at any level of any organization. Along these lines, let me share some wise and encouraging words by Jack Welch:

> "Insecure managers create complexity. Real leaders don't need clutter. People must have the self-confidence to be clear, precise, to be sure that every person in their organization — highest to lowest — understands what the business is trying to achieve. But it's not easy. You can't believe how hard it is for people to be simple, how much they fear being simple. They worry that if they are simple, people will think they are simple-minded. In reality, of course, it's just the reverse. Clear, tough-minded people are the most simple."

In short: if you can become a great Simplifier, you are on track to becoming a great leader. Get started today!

SIMPLICITY FOR SUCCESS BOOK SERIES

As I had explained above, while writing this book, I realized that trying to cover all key aspects and tools of *Simplicity* would result in an 'epic' volume with hundreds of pages. That's counter to the objective of making things simple. Hence, I decided to create the *Simplicity for Success* series, with each volume focused on a particular topic. This approach will:

1. Allow you to determine which topics you want to explore in more depth.
2. Keep each volume very lean and, hence, simple.
3. Allow us to easily update each volume over time.

I sincerely hope that you will appreciate this approach. Future volumes of the *Simplicity for Success* series will help you to address more function-specific business challenges, such as:

- *How to develop your business strategy and plan for success.*
- *How to develop and manage your budget.*

- *How to ensure that you develop the products and services that your customers really want.*
- *How to demonstrate to your customers that you really understand their needs.*
- *How to make the buying process as smooth as possible for your customers.*
- *How to develop and maintain a great relationship with your customers.*
- *How to be smart about buying the things you need to run your business.*
- *How to find great employees, manage them fairly, and make them happy contributors to the success of your business.*

The future volumes of the *Simplicity for Success* series will be developed based on the *Framework of Simplicity Tools* that was introduced in Chapter 4. Sample topics we are planning to cover you find in the below graphic.

The order in which we will write and publish future volumes of the series will also depend on perceived demand. So please share your interests and needs to help us to prioritize.

Meanwhile, if you believe that we could help you, your team, or your company through the application of Simplicity, please also reach out. We also offer courses, seminars, workshops, coaching, and consulting on *Simplicity for Success.*

You can reach us via our website, *www.simplifier.co*, or via email at *info@simplifier.co*.

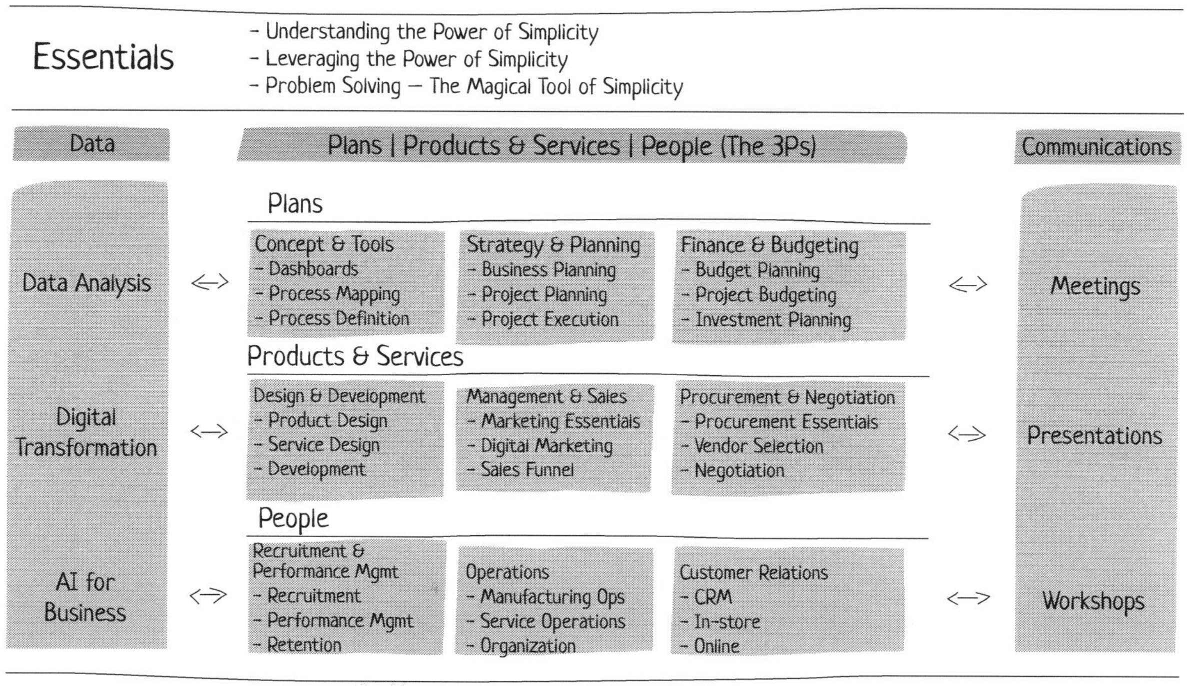

Essentials
- Understanding the Power of Simplicity
- Leveraging the Power of Simplicity
- Problem Solving — The Magical Tool of Simplicity

Data	Plans	Products & Services	People (The 3Ps)	Communications

Plans

Data Analysis <->

Concept & Tools
- Dashboards
- Process Mapping
- Process Definition

Strategy & Planning
- Business Planning
- Project Planning
- Project Execution

Finance & Budgeting
- Budget Planning
- Project Budgeting
- Investment Planning

<-> Meetings

Products & Services

Digital Transformation <->

Design & Development
- Product Design
- Service Design
- Development

Management & Sales
- Marketing Essentials
- Digital Marketing
- Sales Funnel

Procurement & Negotiation
- Procurement Essentials
- Vendor Selection
- Negotiation

<-> Presentations

People

AI for Business <->

Recruitment & Performance Mgmt
- Recruitment
- Performance Mgmt
- Retention

Operations
- Manufacturing Ops
- Service Operations
- Organization

Customer Relations
- CRM
- In-store
- Online

<-> Workshops

FIGURE 13
POTENTIAL FUTURE TOPICS OF THE SIMPLICITY FOR SUCCESS SERIES BASED ON THE FRAMEWORK OF SIMPLICITY TOOLS

SIMPLICITY FACTS
OVERVIEW

1. *Simplicity* is 1% talent and 99% hard work.

2. *Simplicity* is elusive. Over time, everything in nature tends to become more disordered, less structured, and hence, less simple.

3. Simple is hard. (*The Paradox of Simplicity*)

4. Keeping things simple is a constant uphill battle.

5. *Complexity* is the 'evil twin' of Simplicity.

6. The three key indicators of *Complexity* are:
   1. Lack of clear goals and objectives
   2. Ineffective communication
   3. Lack of competence

7. Success is about doing the right thing, not about doing everything right.

8. The simple equation driving every business is:
   Profit = Revenue − Cost;
   you want to maximize Revenue and minimize Cost.

9. The *Virtuous Cycle of Simplicity*:
   Structure − Prioritize − Iterate.

10. *Simplicity* helps you to focus; focus helps you to achieve *Simplicity*.

11. More data does not necessarily result in more relevant insights.

12. To get things 'simple' (yet not 'simplistic'), you need to identify what is essential & meaningful as opposed to what isn't.

13. The *Rule of Three* is so valuable because people can easily remember three things and because it forces prioritization.

14. Creating transparency is one of the most essential keys to *Simplicity* − and typically requires 80% of the overall effort.

15. The *80:20 Rule* is based on the observation that the lion's share of the effect comes from a relatively small number of causes.

16. To be able to effectively conduct an analysis, the necessary data:
    1. Needs to exist
    2. Needs to be easily accessible
    3. Should not require much preparation
       (e.g., cleansing)

SIMPLICITY TIPS
OVERVIEW

1. A picture is worth a thousand words, so use images, graphs, and charts a lot.

2. In your quest to leverage *Simplicity* for success, make ample use of your Common Sense.

3. Make *Simplicity* an 'obsession.'

4. Simplify by standardizing wherever you can — your colleagues and customers will love you for it!

5. In data analyses, always keep this law of computer science in mind: Garbage in, garbage out!

6. Simply doing the most important thing is always the most important thing.

7. Problem structuring needs to follow 3 steps:
   1. Structure and review all available data
   2. Generate a fact-based hypothesis
   3. Identify the key questions to prove or disprove your hypothesis

8. When structuring problems, make things MECE
   (*Mutually Exclusive, Collectively Exhaustive*).

9. Try to make all things come in Threes.

10. To prioritize your analyses, do three things
    simultaneously:
    1. Keep looking at the *Big Picture*
    2. Identify (and prioritize) the *Key Drivers*
    3. Apply the 80:20 *Rule*

11. Don't try to be precise in business analyses —
    make analyses easier to grasp
    by rounding numbers.

12. To be able to more efficiently derive SoWhats,
    create graphs (e.g., bar charts)
    rather than tables.

13. Always try to use the 80:20 Rule to prioritize and
    identify *low-hanging fruits*.

14. Sanity check every analysis for plausibility before
    you start to try to identify SoWhats.

15. Create storylines and presentations that follow the
    Top-down Approach.

16. If you need an executive decision, provide options,
    along with pros & cons for each, and recommend
    which option to pursue.

17. For every-day decisions, provide simple rules.

ACKNOWLEDGMENTS

There have been countless people who have influenced and inspired me over the years. In one way or the other, they have all contributed to the creation of this book. Thank you all!

Special mentions are required for:

- My most influential teachers, mentors, and colleagues — many of them I am proud to call my friends — who provided me with various inspirations. Their generosity and spirit are reflected throughout this book:
  - The late Arthur C. Clarke, Harry O. Ruppe, Hermann Oberth, and H. Hermann Koelle.
  - Andy Aldrin, Axel Krieger, Bernd Zabel, Bill Meehan, Bob Dvorak, Buzz Aldrin, Guenter Rommel, Harald Bauer, Jim Wertz, Johannes Pruchnow, Klaus Voormann, Lothar Stein, Nicole Boyer, Oliver Kharraz, Roby Stancel, Ron Bancroft, Ron Ashkenas, Todd Edebohls, Tom Hutton, Uli Naeher, Volker Gruentges, Wilhelm Rall, Wiley Larson, Will Bachman.
- My friends who generously took time to review draft versions of this book and provide tons of

invaluable feedback: Bershu Nkwawir, Carlos Entrena Utrilla, CJ Johansen, Dagmar Saschek, Devra DeAngelis, Jean Bigoney, Michaela Ballek, Pete Tunnicliffe, Sven Beiker, and Thomas Dittler.

- Ken Segall, a true pioneer of *Simplicity*, for his kind permission to use some of his quotes.
- Daniela Chervenkova and Andrey Chervenkov for the excellent layout and Herby Utz for his great advice along these lines.

Above all, I would like to thank my wonderful wife, Noushin, and my darling son, Daniel. You are my everything. Thank you for putting up with a crazy-driven husband and dad. I could have never done this without you. Love you, bistopanjda!

About the Author

Peter Eckart is a rocket scientist-turned-McKinsey-consultant-turned-senior-executive-turned-Simplifier.

He has been reporting into and advising CxO-level management for over 20 years. Passionate about creating impact, and a believer in the power of Simplicity, he has worked for major corporations, family businesses, SMEs, and start-ups (early stage to unicorn), as well as academia and government, across three continents.

Peter is the Founder and Managing Partner of Simplifier Inc. and Advisor & Lecturer at the Aldrin Space Institute.

He holds a Ph.D. in Space Engineering and a Masters in Aerospace Engineering from Technical University of Munich, Germany.

Peter currently resides in Palo Alto, CA, with his wife and son.

REFERENCES

Simplicity Books

Ashkenas, Ron
Simply Effective
Harvard Business Review
Press, 2009

Collinson, Simon; Jay, Melvin
*From Complexity to
Simplicity:
Unleash Your Organization's
Potential*
Palgrave Macmillan, 2012

Jensen, Bill
*Simplicity: The New
Competitive Advantage*
Perseus Books, 2000

Jensen, Bill
*The Simplicity Survival
Handbook*
Perseus Books, 2003

Kluger, Jeffrey
Simplexity
Hyperion, 2009

Koch, Richard; Lockwood, Greg
*Simplify: How the Best
Businesses in the World
Succeed*
Entrepreneur Press, 2016

Maeda, John
The Laws of Simplicity
The MIT Press, 2006

Scherer, Jiri; Hartschen,
Michael; Bruegger, Chris
Simplicity for Business Success
GABAL Verlag, Germany, 2011

Segall, Ken
*Insanely Simple: The
Obsession that Drives Apple's
Success*
Portfolio, 2013

Segall, Ken
*Think Simple: How Smart
Leaders Defeat Complexity*
Portfolio, 2016

Siegel, Alan
*Simple – Conquering the
Crisis of Complexity*
Twelve, 2013

in a Complex World
Mariner Books, 2016
Houghton Mifflin Harcourt,
2015

Sull, Donald;
Eisenhardt, Kathleen
Simple Rules: How to Thrive

Trout, Jack
The Power of Simplicity
McGraw-Hill, 1999

Top 60 Business Books of All Time – A Subjective List
(Note: This list generally references the latest publications,
not necessarily the 'originals')

Beckwith, Harry
*Selling the Invisible:
A Field Guide to Modern
Marketing*
Warner Books, 1997

Bedbury, Scott;
Fenichell, Stephen
A New Brand World
Penguin Books, 2003

Berman, Karen; Knight, Joe
Financial Intelligence
Harvard Business Review
Press, 2006

Blanchard, Kenneth
The One Minute Manager
William Morrow and
Company, 1982

Bossidy, Larry; Charan, Ram
*Execution: The Discipline of
Getting Things Done*
Currency, 2002

Buckingham, Marcus;
Coffman, Curt
First Break All the Rules
Brilliance Audio, 1999

Carnegie, Dale
*How To Win Friends and
Influence People*
Simon & Schuster, 2009

Charan, Ram
*What the CEO Wants You to Know:
How Your Company Really Works*
Currency, 2017

Christensen, Clayton
The Innovators Dilemma
Harvard Business Review
Press, 1997

Collins, Jim
*Good to Great: Why Some
Companies Make the Leap. . .
And Others Don't*
Harper Business, 2001

Covey, Steven R.
*The 7 Habits of Highly
Effective People: Powerful
Lessons in Personal Change*
Free Press, 1989

Cunningham, Lawrence A.
*The Essays of Warren Buffet:
Lessons for Investors &
Managers*
John Wiley & Sons, 2013

De Bono, Edward
Six Thinking Hats
Little, Brown & Company, 1985

Deming, W. Edwards
Out of the Crisis
MIT Press, 1982

Drucker, Peter
The Effective Executive
Harper Business, 1966

Drucker, Peter
*The Essential Drucker: The
Best of Sixty Years of Peter
Drucker's Essential Writings
on Management*
Harper Business, 2008

Foster, Richard; Kaplan, Sarah
Creative Destruction
Crown Business, 2001

Gitomer, Jeffrey
*The Sales Bible: The Ultimate
Sales Resource: Including The 10. 5
Commandments of Sales Success*
William Morrow, 1994

Gladwell, Malcolm
Outliers — The Story of Success
Little, Brown & Company, 2008

Gladwell, Malcolm
The Tipping Point
Abacus, 2002

Godin, Seth
Purple Cow
Penguin UK, 2005

Goldratt, Eliyahu M.; Cox, Jeff
*The Goal: A Process of
Ongoing Improvement*
North River Press, 1984

Goleman, Daniel
*Emotional Intelligence: Why It
Matters More Than IQ*
Bantam Books, 1995

Greenwald, Bruce; Kahn, Judd
Competition Demystified
Penguin USA, 2007

Hamel, Gary; Prahalad, C. K.
Competing for the Future
Harvard Business School
Press, 1994

Hammer, Michael; Champy,
James A.
*Reengineering the
Corporation*
Harper Business, 1993

Hill, Napoleon
Think and Grow Rich
Sound Wisdom, 2019

Hill, Napoleon
The Law of Success in Sixteen Lessons
Value Classic Reprints, 2018

Kahneman, Daniel
Thinking, Fast and Slow
Farrar, Straus & Giroux, 2011

Kaplan, Robert S.;
Norton, David P.
The Balanced Scorecard: Translating Strategy into Action
Harvard Business Review Press, 1996

Katzenbach, Jon R.;
Smith, Douglas K.
The Wisdom of Teams: Creating the High-Performance Organization
Harvard Business Review Press, 1992

Kawasaki, Guy
The Art of the Start: The Time-Tested, Battle-Hardened Guide for Anyone Starting Anything
Penguin, 2004

Kelley, Tom;
Littman, Jonathan
The Art of Innovation: Lessons in Creativity from IDEO, America's Leading Design Firm
Currency, 2001

Kim, W. Chan; Mauborgne, Renée
Blue Ocean Strategy
Harvard Business Review Press, 2004

Koch, Richard
The 80/20 Principle: The Secret to Achieving More with Less
Currency, 1999

Kotter, John P.
Leading Change
Harvard Business Review Press, 1988

Lencioni, Patrick
Five Dysfunctions of a Team
Jossey-Bass, 2002

Liker, Jeffrey K
The Toyota Way
McGraw-Hill Education, 2004

Magretta, Joan
What Management Is
Harper Collins Business, 2002

Mandino, Og
The Greatest Salesman in the World
Bantam, 1983

McKinsey & Company Inc.
(Tim Koller, Marc Goedhart, David Wessels)
Valuation: Measuring and Managing the Value of Companies
John Wiley & Sons, 1990

Minto, Barbara
The Pyramid Principle
Prentice-Hall, 2010

Moore, Geoffrey A
Crossing the Chasm
Harper Business, 2017

Neumeier, Marty
*Zag: The Number One Strategy
of High-Performance Brands*
New Riders, 2006

Osterwalder, Alexander;
Pigneur, Yves
Business Model Generation
Wiley, 2011

Pande, Peter S.; Neuman,
Robert P., Cavanagh Roland
R., et al.
The 6-Sigma Way
McGraw-Hill Education, 2000

Pfeffer, Jeffrey; Sutton, Robert
The Knowing-Doing Gap
Harvard Business School
Press, 1999

Pine II, B. Joseph; Gilmore,
James H.
The Experience Economy
Harvard Business Review
Press, 1999

Porter, Michael E.
*Competitive Strategy:
Techniques for Analysing
Industries and Competitors*
Free Press, 1998

Reynolds, Garr
*Presentation Zen: Simple
Ideas on Presentation Design
and Delivery*
New Riders, 2011

Ries, Al; Trout, Jack
*The 22 Immutable
Laws of Marketing:
Violate Them at
Your Own Risk!*
Harper Business, 1994

Ries, Eric
*The Lean Start-up:
How Today's
Entrepreneurs Use
Continuous Innovation to
Create Radically
Successful Businesses*
Currency, 2011

Schwartz, David J.
The Magic of Thinking Big
Simon & Schuster, 2011

Schwartz, Peter
The Art of the Long View
Crown Business, 1996

Senge, Peter
*The Fifth Discipline:
The Art and Practice of the
Learning Organization*
Currency, 1990

Stack, Jack
*The Great Game of
Business*
Currency, 1992

Surowiecki, James
The Wisdom of Crowds
Doubleday, 2004

Thiel, Peter
From Zero to One
Currency, 2014

Townsend, Robert
Up Your Business
John Wiley & Sons, 1970

Tracy, Brian
*Focal Point: A Proven System
to Simplify Your Life, Double
Your Productivity, and
Achieve All Your Goals*
AMACOM, 2001

Wing, R. L.
The Art of Strategy
Main Street Books, 1988